STEP BY STEP DRAWING

ZOO ANIMALS

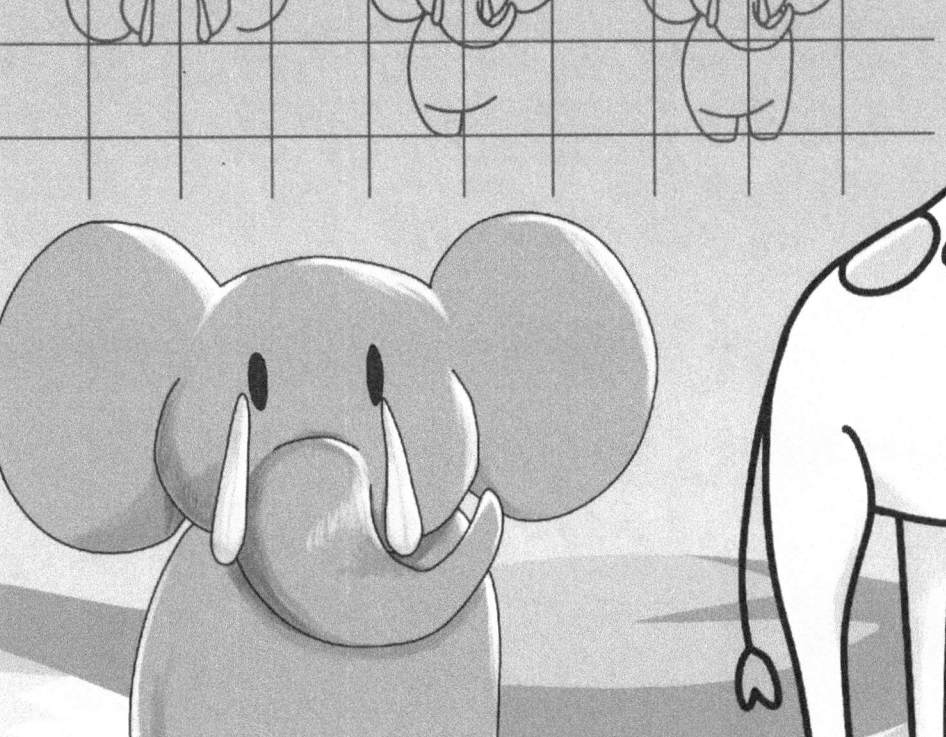

Miriam R. Ahumada

for kids

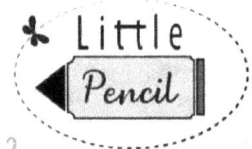

CONTENTS

STEP BY STEP

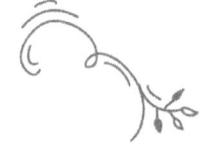

Published by: Little Pencil
hello@littlepencilpress.com

This is to Qinni art, whose art inspired and continues to inspire me wherever she is.

INTRODUCTION

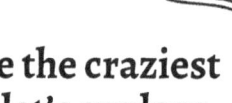

Since we were all kids, going to the zoo seemed like the craziest and most fun adventure we could go on, this time let's explore these Zoo Animals together!

Step by Step guide is the easiest way to learn how to draw and to let your imagination wander. I'm here to let you know how to make the basics and the main structure of your drawings, how to make every line and angle work, and everything else that follows will flow smoothly and accordingly just how you want it to be.

Hey, if it doesn't exactly looks like in your head, don't beat yourself up. Every developed skill needs practice, be patient, practice, but most of all,

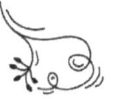 **HAVE FUN!**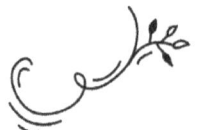

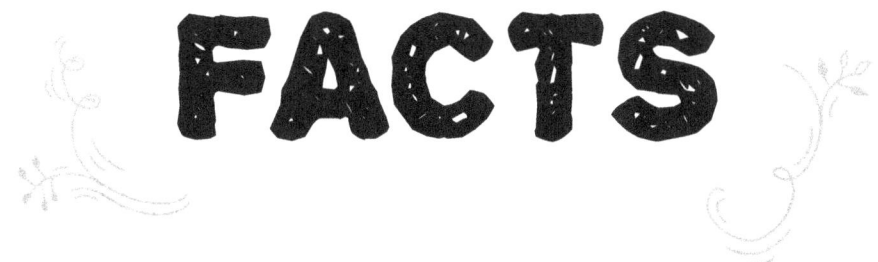

FACTS

WHAT IS THE ZOO?

Zoos are home to many animals around the world that live in habitats instead of the wild.

WHAT IS A HABITAT?

Habitats are exhibits where the zoo tries to recreate where the animals use to live.

WHAT ARE SOME TYPES OF HABITATS?

Some of these habitats include grassy plains, deserts and rainforests.

WHY ARE ZOOS IMPORTANT?

Zoos study animals so that we can learn more about them, what they eat, behave or if needed, the treatment or medicine to get healthier. Zoos also protect and help take care of animals that are extinct or disappearing from the wild.

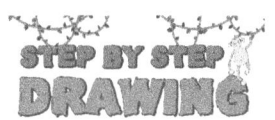

WHAT IS THE BIGGEST ZOO?

The Red McCombs Wildlife in Texas with its 12,000 acres (4856.2277 ha).

WHAT ANIMAL SPECIES HAVE BEEN SAVED BY THE ZOOS?

Arabian Oryx, Przewalski's Horse, California Condor, Bongo, Golden Frog, and Golden Lion Tamarin.

WHAT ARE THE DIFFERENT TYPES OF BEARS YOU CAN FIND AT THE ZOO?

Grizzly bear, Polar bear, Panda bear, American bear and Spectacled bear.

WHAT IS THE BIGGEST BEAR?

The biggest bear is the Polar bear

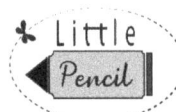 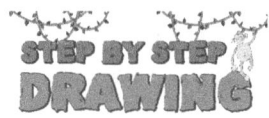

WHAT BEAR USED TO BE MISTAKEN BY A RACCOON RELATIVE?

The Panda bear! Their spotted eyes and black and white fur looks a little like the raccoons'.

WHAT IS THE TALLEST ANIMAL YOU CAN FIND AT A ZOO?

The giraffe, and they are not only the tallest at the zoo but the tallest in the world!

HOW LONG CAN A TURTLE LIVE?

The Galapagos Turtles can live up to 100 years!

WHAT IS THE BRIGHTEST BIRD?

The flamingo has pink, red and orange-ish feathers in its whole body, meanwhile other colorful birds have bright and dark feathers.

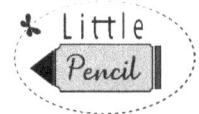
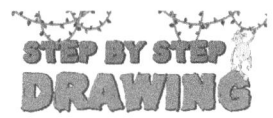

WHAT MAKES FLAMINGO FEATHERS PINK?

Their colors come from the foods they eat, like algae and small crabs, shrimp, crayfish, and more.

WHY DO IGUANAS SUNBATHE?

Iguanas are cold blooded, so they like to lay on the sun to warm their bodies.

WHAT IS THE DIFFERENCE BETWEEN A CROCODILE AND AN ALLIGATOR?

When an alligator closes its mouth his fourth tooth fits inside its mouth and a crocodile's fourth tooth sticks out!

WHAT SIMILARITIES DO AN ALLIGATOR HAVE TO A DOG?

Both open their mouths to release heat.

 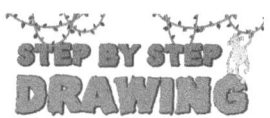

WHAT IS THE BIGGEST ANIMAL YOU CAN FIND AT THE ZOO?

The elephant! and not only is it the biggest animal you can find at the zoo, it's the biggest animal you can find in land!

HOW MUCH DOES AN ELEPHANT WEIGH?

Adult African elephants are huge. Some can weigh as much as a school bus.

WHAT IS A GROUP OF LIONS CALLED?

Lions live in groups and they are called prides.

HOW MUCH DOES A LION SLEEP?

Lions can sleep up to 21 hours each day.

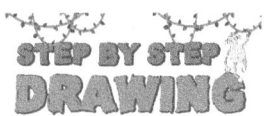

ANIMAL DESCRIPTIONS

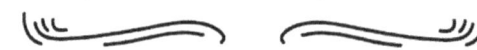

ALLIGATOR

Alligators are reptiles, which means that they are cold-blooded. Their whole bodies are covered with dry skin and scales. They can weigh over 800 pounds and grow as long as 10 to 13 feet. They are usually very dark green or black in color. Alligators are predators and eat meat.

CHEETAH

Cheetahs are big cats with black and gold spotted fur, sometimes they are mistaken for jaguars, but their spots are rounded, and they have long black lines that run from their eyes to their mouth called tears. They are the fastest mammal in the world, that makes them great hunters.

LION

Lions are part of the big cat family; they are the only cats that live in groups called pride. Their roar is so powerful it can be heard from five miles away. Female lions are the ones in charge of hunting, male lions stay back and guard the territory and the cubs.

IGUANA

Iguanas are reptiles that can grow up to 6 feet and 20 pounds but most of their length is their tail. They are mostly herbivores eating plants and fruit but sometimes they'll eat small insects or eggs. Iguanas are excellent swimmers, if their tail gets cut off, they can grow a new one!.

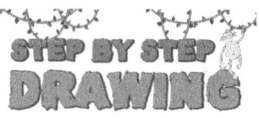

FLAMINGO

Flamingos are large pink birds and even though they seem big, they weigh only 5 to 6 pounds. They have a distinctive pose because they like to stand on one foot. They live long lives 30 to 50 years.

GIRAFFE

Giraffes are the tallest animals in the world, males can grow to 18 feet and females to 14 feet. Their height and excellent eyesight helps them lookout for predators. Giraffes are herbivores, their favorite tree is the Acacia tree, they use their long necks and growing tongue to reach the top leaves.

PANDA

Pandas have black and white fur, always two black patches around their eyes. Even though Pandas are born just a few inches long and about 100 grams, they grow up more than 300 pounds. Pandas eat only bamboo and they eat 22 pounds a day!

PARROT

Parrots are bright-colored birds with curved beaks and clawed feet. Parrots are believed to be amongst the most intelligent bird species. Most of them rely on seeds as their main food source but they also sometimes eat fruit, flowers, and small insects.

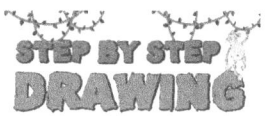

SLOTH

Sloths are medium mammals that grow to 23 inches. There are 2 types of sloths: ones that have 3 toes and ones that have 2 toes. Sloths are known to be lazy but the reason they are slow is that they have four-patched stomachs that make digestion very slow, leaving them with little energy to move around.

SNAKE

Snakes are reptiles and they don't have eyelids, ears, arms, or legs. They have long and slender bodies and their skin is covered in scales. They can taste scents with their tongue when they flick them in and out. Snakes don't have a voice, but they can hiss. Because snakes are cold-blooded, they like warm weather.

TIGER

Tigers are the biggest species of the cat family; they grow to 11 feet and weigh 660 pounds. They are really agile animals being great swimmers and can swim up to almost 4 miles. A group of tigers is called an ambush.

ZEBRA

Zebras are relatives of the horses or donkeys; they have unique patterns of black and white stripes. They have excellent eyesight and hearing, leaving them always alert to predators.

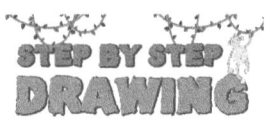

WALRUS

Walruses are huge marine mammals and are known as the "Giants" or "Kings" of the arctic. They grow up to be 11.5 feet in size and can weigh up 3,000 pounds. Walruses have large tusks that they use to cut through ice as well as to defend themselves. They are social and stay in groups called "herds".

HIPPO

Hippopotamus means "River horse" it's a large mammal that is known to be very protective of their territory, making them aggressive and dangerous with outsiders. They have short legs, very wide mouths, and bodies that are shaped like barrels. They stay in the water during the day to stay cool and once the sun goes down, they go into the land to look for food, mainly grass (they are herbivores).

KANGAROO

Kangaroos are designed to jump with two powerful back legs and a strong long tail that helps them jump around and keep their balance. They can grow to be between 5 and 6 feet and weigh between 50 and 120 pounds. Kangaroos have babies called "Joeys," and they carry them on their belly pouch for 8 months until they are ready to stand and jump on their own.

PENGUIN

Penguins are birds that have black and white plumage for camouflage, black in their backs to not be seen from above and white on their fronts to seem like it's the sun reflecting seen from below. Penguins are birds that don't fly, they adapted their "wings" into flippers to help them slide and swim better. Penguins eat fish and other sea life creatures.

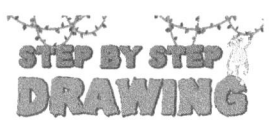

POLAR BEAR

Polar bears are big mammals that have black skin and transparent hair that makes it seem like its white fur. They are the largest carnivore that lives on land, their diet consists mostly of seals. Males can weigh up to 1500 pounds and females the half of that. They are great swimmers and spend most of their time at sea.

TOUCAN

Toucan is a bird with colorful bills, its length is 8 inches and it's very light, and not very strong, despite its size. They live together in small flocks and nests in hollow trees. They are very noisy and get to live up to 20 years.

TREE FROG

Tree Frogs are amphibians that come in all sorts of color and sizes. They have sticky toes that help them climb better and be great jumpers. They spend almost all of the time up in trees, their colors help them camouflage themselves from predators.

TURTLE

Turtles are reptiles that have hard shells that help them shield themselves, it's called "carapace." Like other reptiles, turtles are coldblooded and like to sunbathe to get warm. Turtles are one of the oldest species to roam the world, around 215 million years.

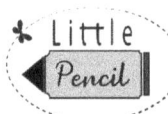
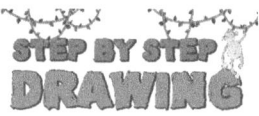

MONKEY

Monkeys are mammals, part of the primate family. There are over 260 different species of monkey around the world, most of them are omnivore, that means that they eat fruit, leaves, nuts, and insects. Monkeys live both on land and on trees and their limbs and thumbs help them swing through trees.

ELEPHANT

Elephants are the biggest living animals on land and weigh between 5,000 to 14,000 pounds. There are two types in the world, the African elephant and the Asian elephant, you can tell them apart by their body size and ear size, the African elephant is bigger in both aspects. They are herbivores and spend almost 16 hours of their day eating.

GIANT ANTEATER

Giant Anteater is the only mammal that has no teeth. They are the largest animal that eats ants, their length is around 79 inches and weigh 90 pounds. Because they have no teeth, they use their long muzzle, foreclaws, and sticky tongue to hunt the ants and insects they eat.

KINKAJOU

The kinkajou is a small mammal also known as the "honey bear." Some people believe they are an endangered species, but they are not! They are just seldom seen because of their strict nocturnal habits. It has large eyes, small ears, short legs with five toes on each foot and a prehensile tail that helps them grab things.

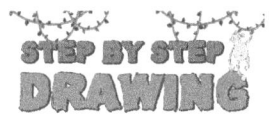

PUMA

Pumas are part of the big cats' family even though they can't roar. They are solitary and nocturnal animals but sometimes they stick together to defend themselves against other animals. Pumas are mainly tan colored and can group up to be 9 feet long.

ADDAX

Addaxes are antelopes and they are part of the horse family; their builds and mane are alike. Both females and males have horns that can be 3 feet long, which they use to protect themselves. They have short grey-brown fur in the winter, and it fades during the summertime turning white.

GORILLA

Gorillas are the largest primates, the males grow to around 5.5 feet tall and weigh around 400 pounds, females are half that size. They are mostly herbivores meaning they eat leaves, stems, fruit, and bamboo but sometimes they will eat insects, especially ants. Gorillas have long limbs and walk on fours using their knuckles.

HARBOR SEAL

Harbor Seals are brown, tan, or grey with short flippers and rounded head, they grow to be 6 feet long and 290 pounds. Harbor Seals are carnivorous eating fish, shrimp, or squids. Harbor Seals are known to be curious but prefer to be in quiet unpopulated areas.

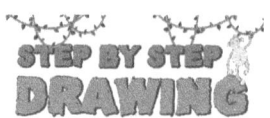

Stop right there!

Scan this code, to get FREE goodies from the Step by Step Book Series!

littlepencilpress.com

TWO WAYS TO WORK WITH THIS BOOK, CHOOSE THE ONE YOU LIKE THE MOST!

HAVE FUN DRAWING!

Simply draw the darker lines and ignore the geometrical shapes, we show you the Step by Step for every drawing.

OR

IMPROVE YOUR DRAWING TECHNIQUE!

Follow every step, starting with the geometrical shapes in a lighter line and over those, draw with darker lines your final animal. With practice, this technique will help you draw anything you want, simply starting by geometrical lines will help you visualize how the final image will look in your drawing area and the traces you will need to create something amazing!

REMEMBER! IF YOU FIND THIS BOOK TOO EASY OR TOO HARD TO FOLLOW, WE HAVE OTHER STEP BY STEP BOOKS WITH DIFFERENT LEVELS OF DIFFICULTY.

DIFFICULTY LEVELS FROM EASIEST TO HARDEST:

1 Step by Step Drawing Zoo Animals

2 Step by Step Ocean Animals

3 Step by Step Fat pets

4 Step by Step Forest Animals

5 Step by Step Cute Mythical Creatures

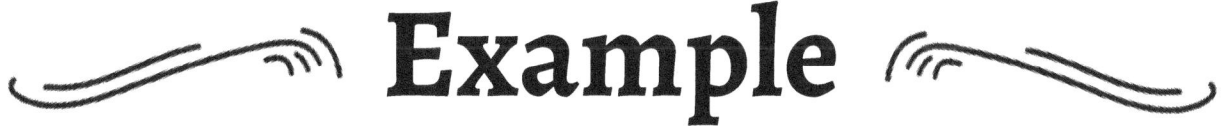# Example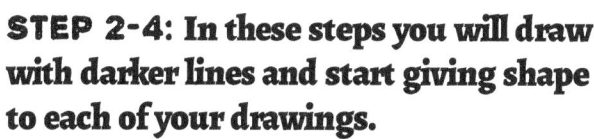

STEP 1: Simplify in geometrical figures the shape of the animal. Remember this will be your guide and over those lines, you will draw your masterpiece so, make them lighter.

STEP 2-4: In these steps you will draw with darker lines and start giving shape to each of your drawings.

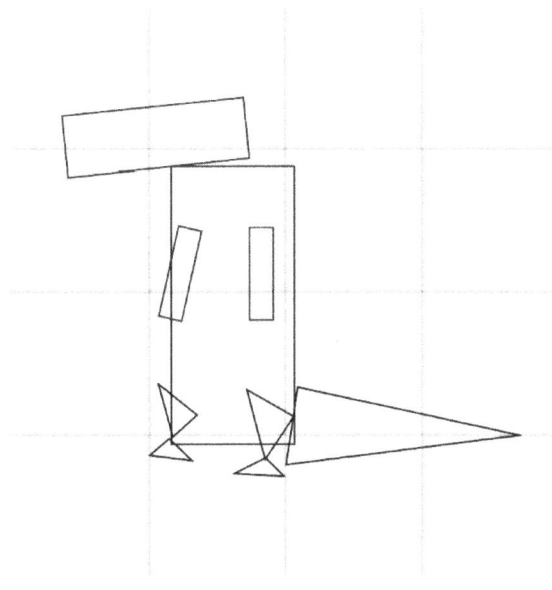

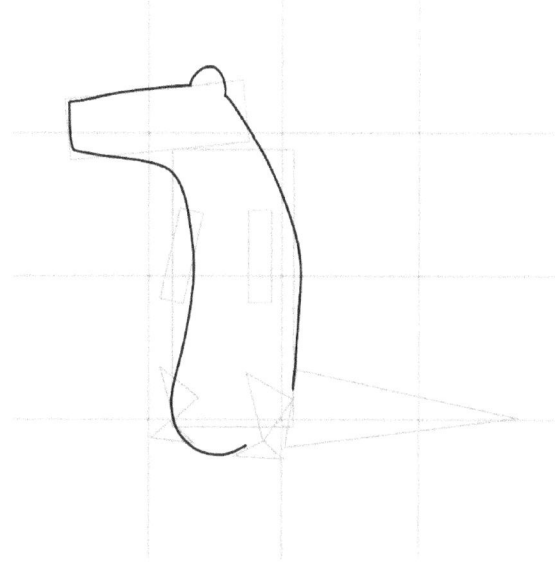

STEP 5: Add details! Now that you have your final shape, we need to add details that will make your drawing look amazing, you can add way more details than the ones we show. Always remember practice makes perfect and you can always redraw what you didn't like but you can never love what you never draw. Be creative!

STEP 6: To finish up your art you just need to erase your geometrical lines and everything else you do not like, add shading if you want and you are done!

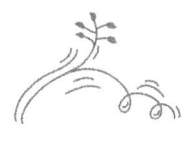

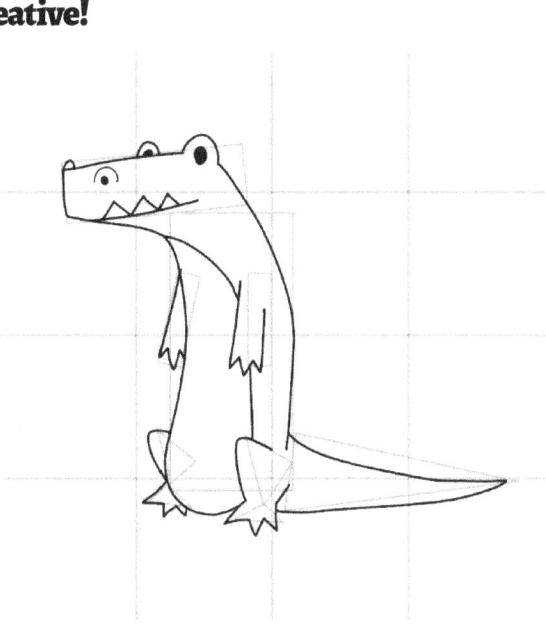

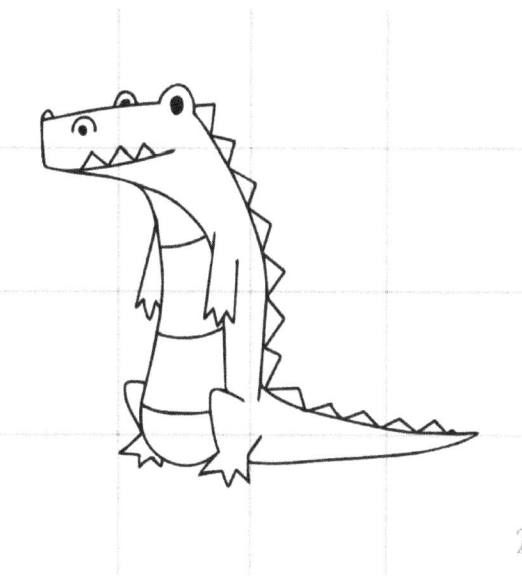

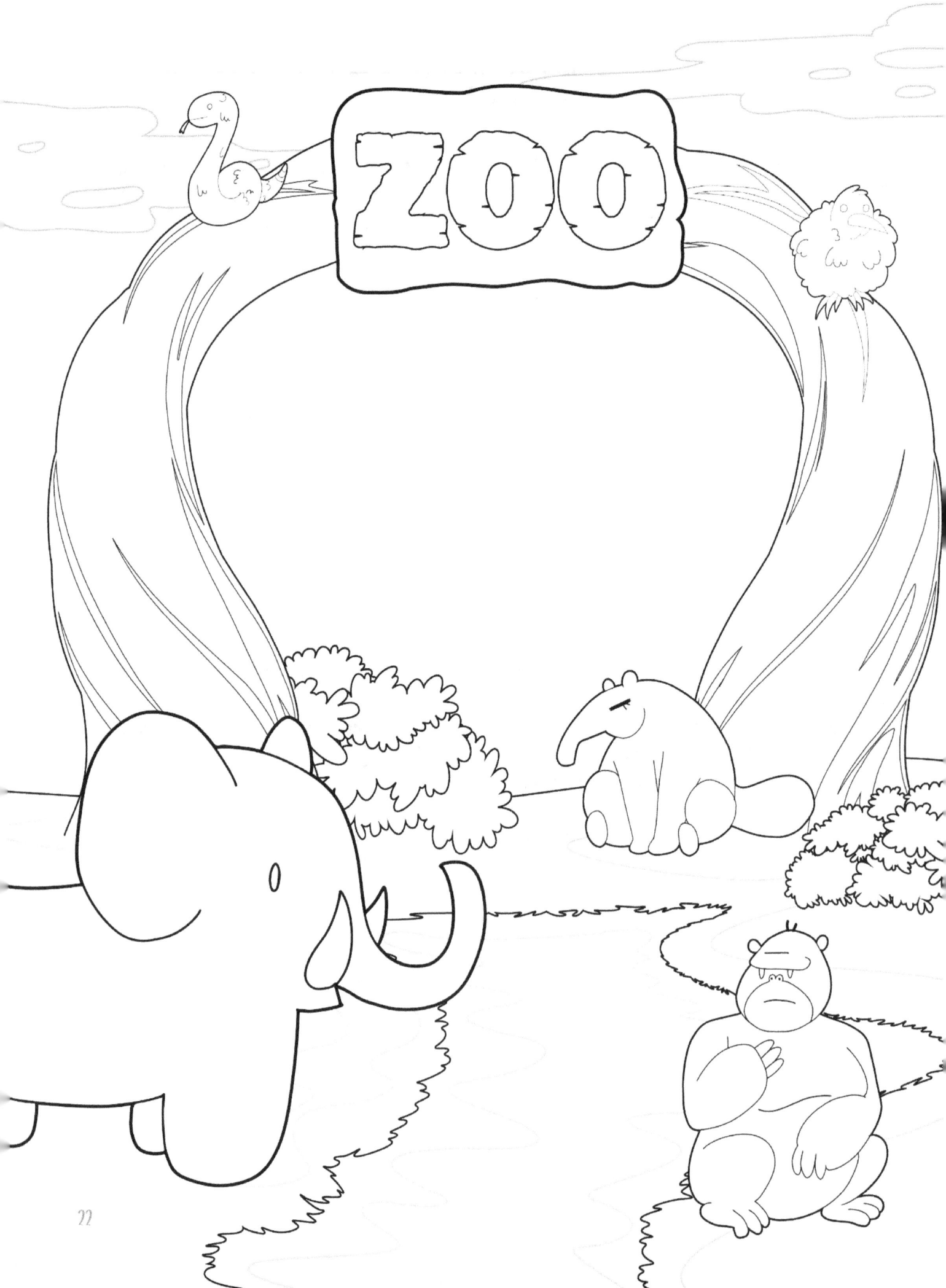

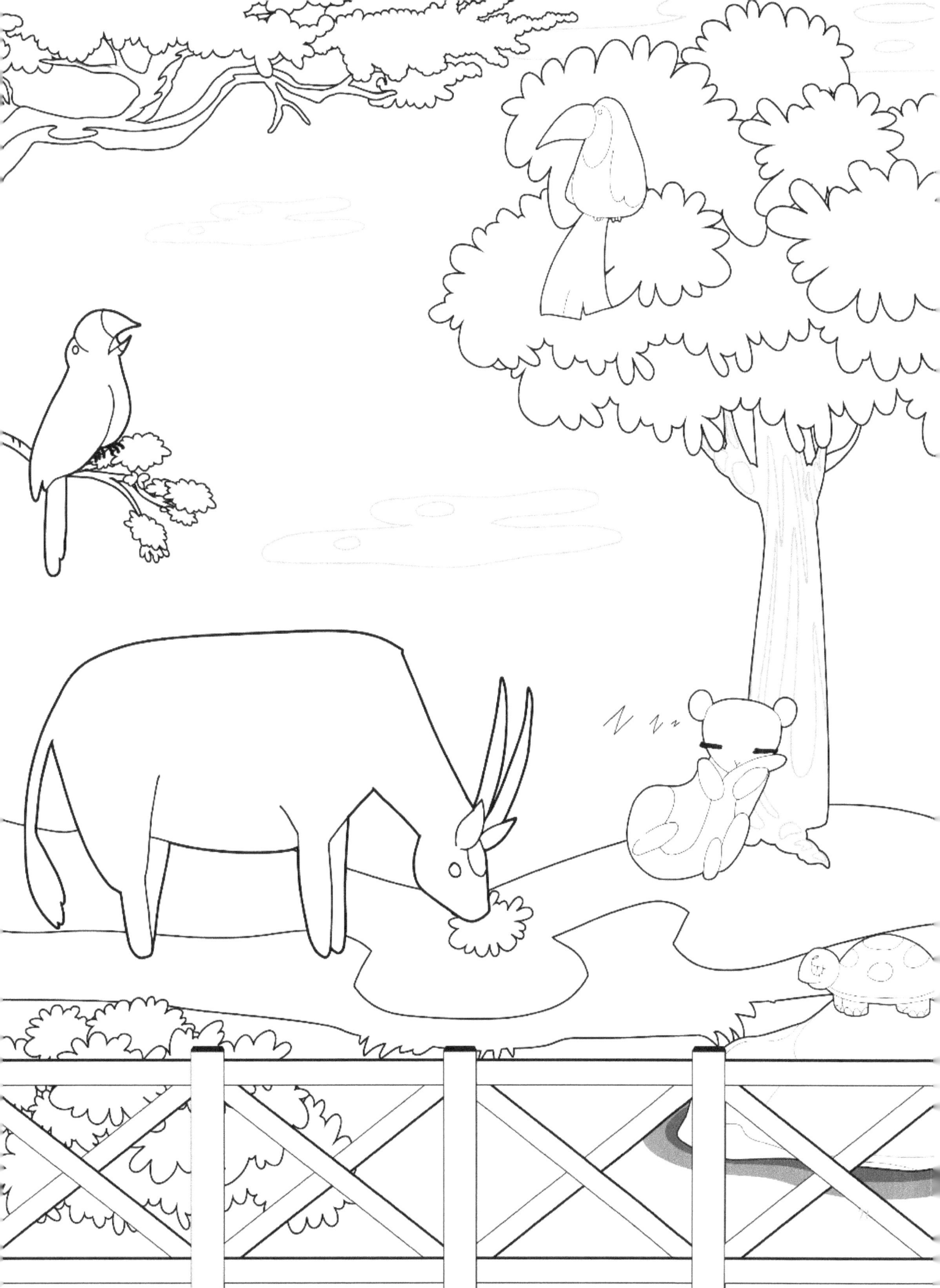

ALLIGATOR

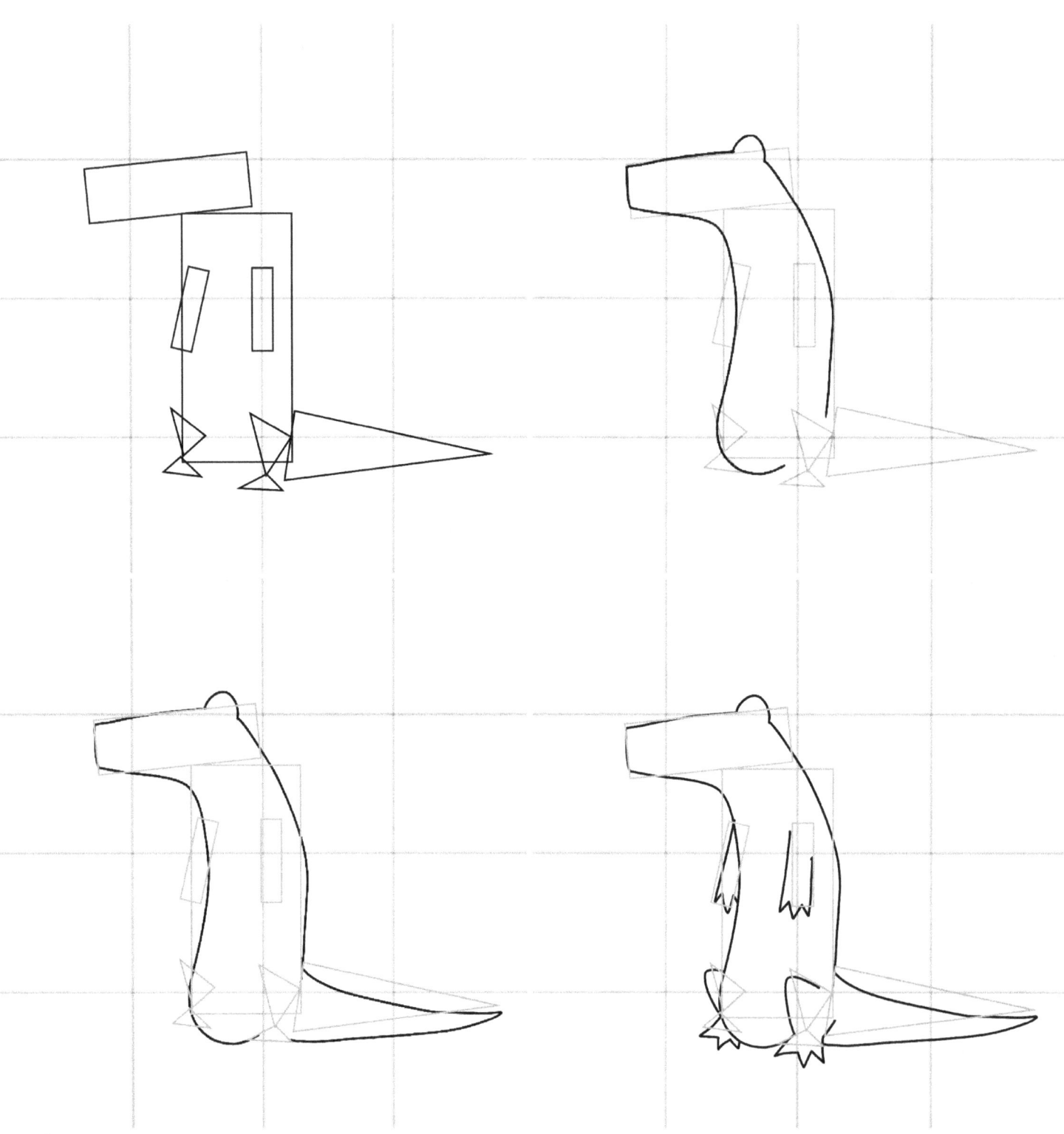

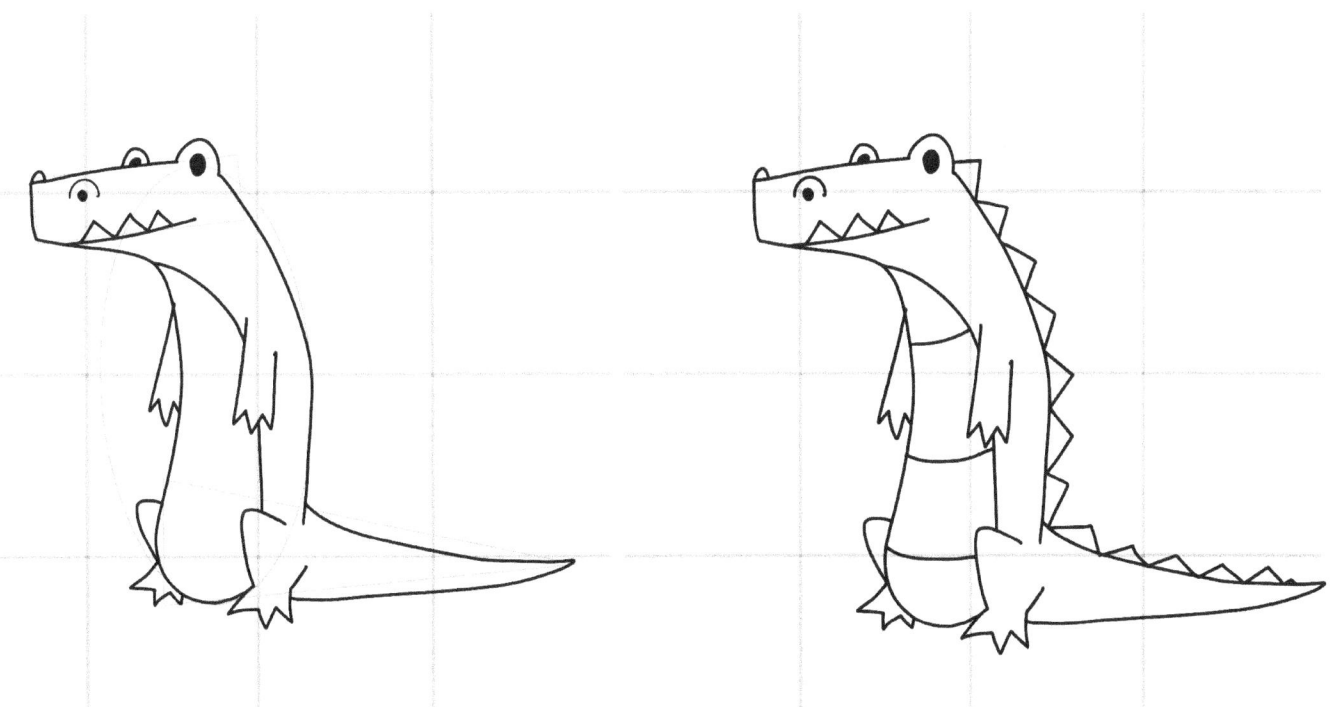

TRY it HERE!

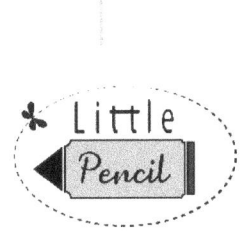

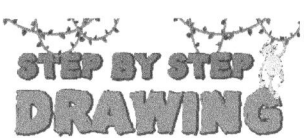

ALLIGATOR

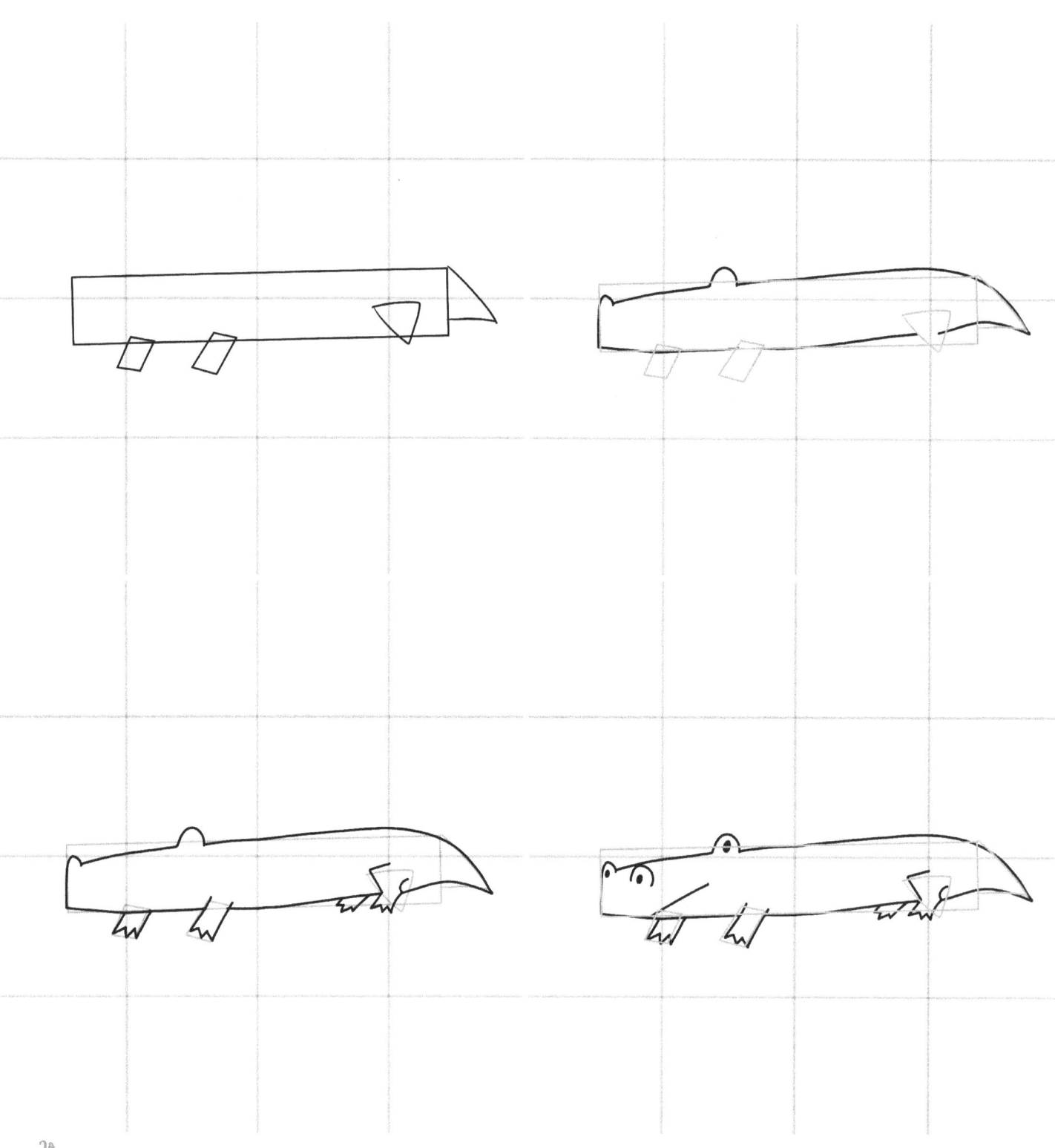

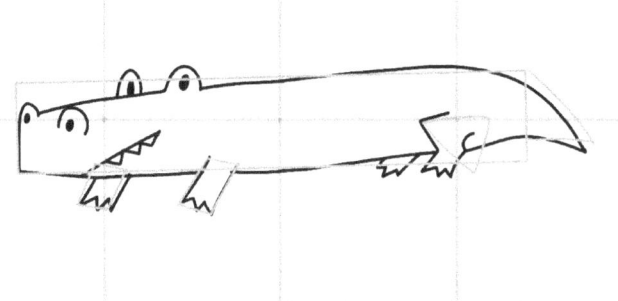 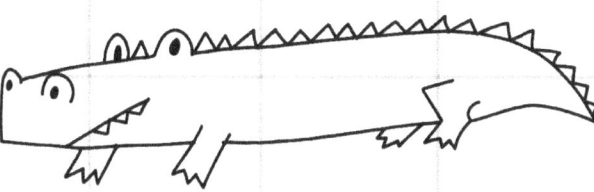

TRY iT HERE!

 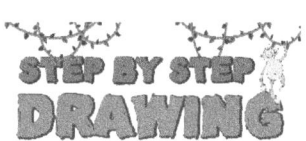

ALLIGATOR

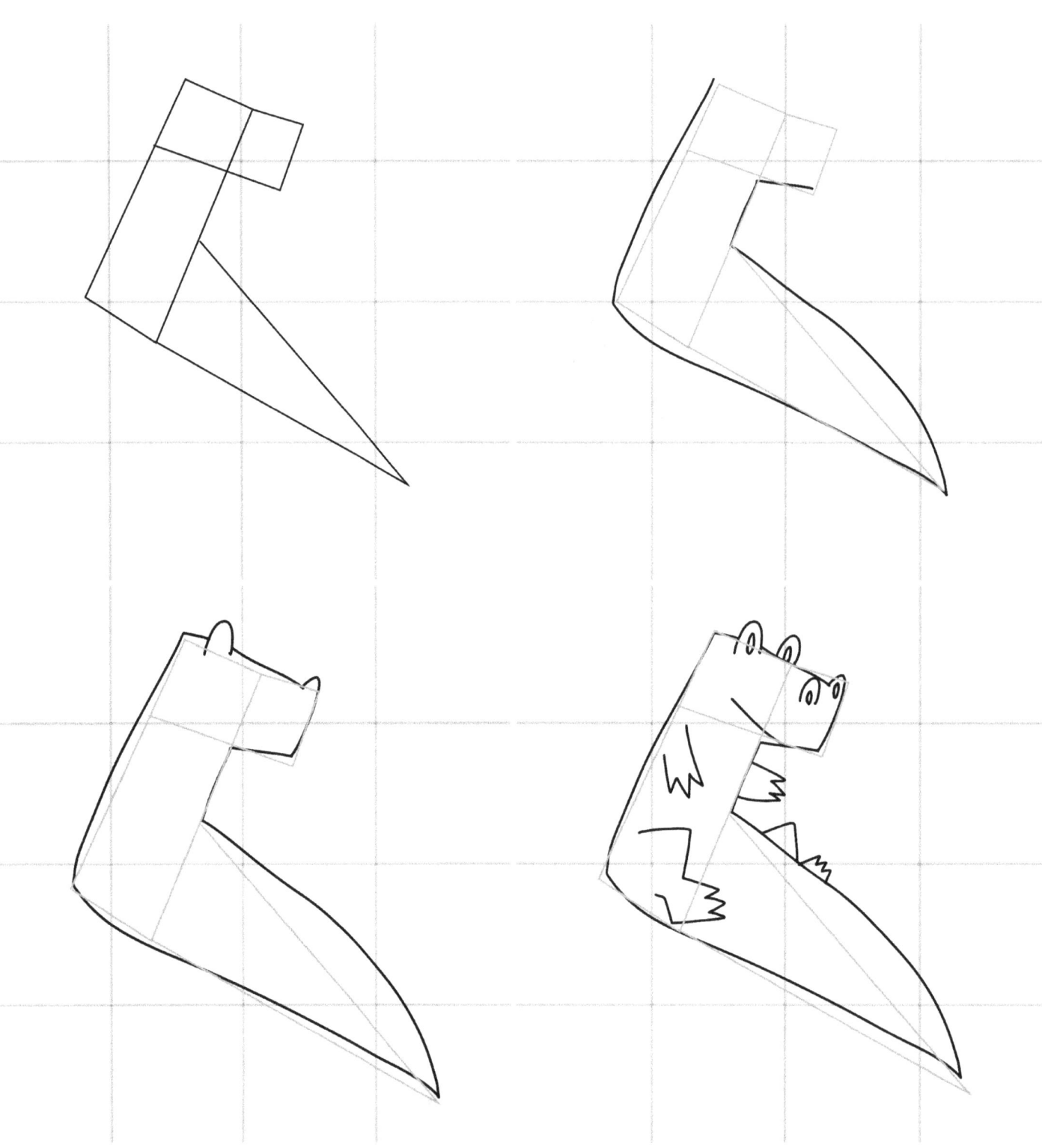

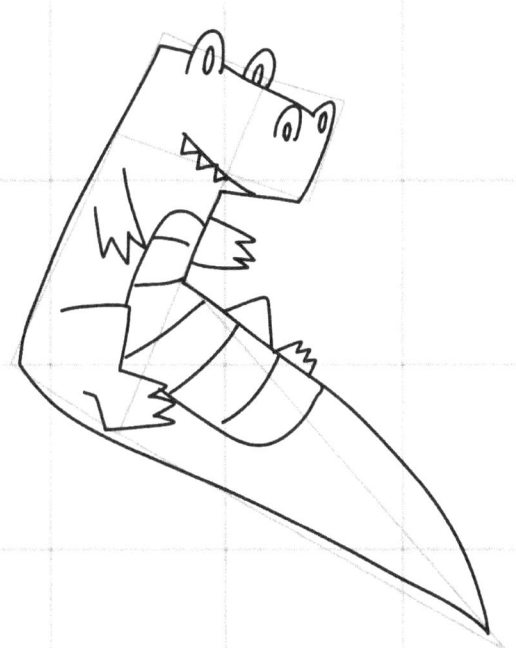
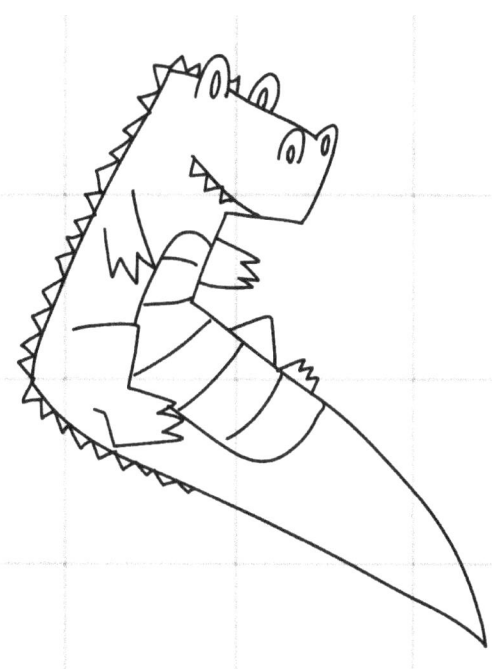

TRY it HERE!

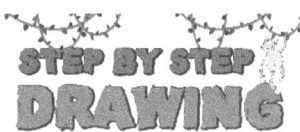

Bison

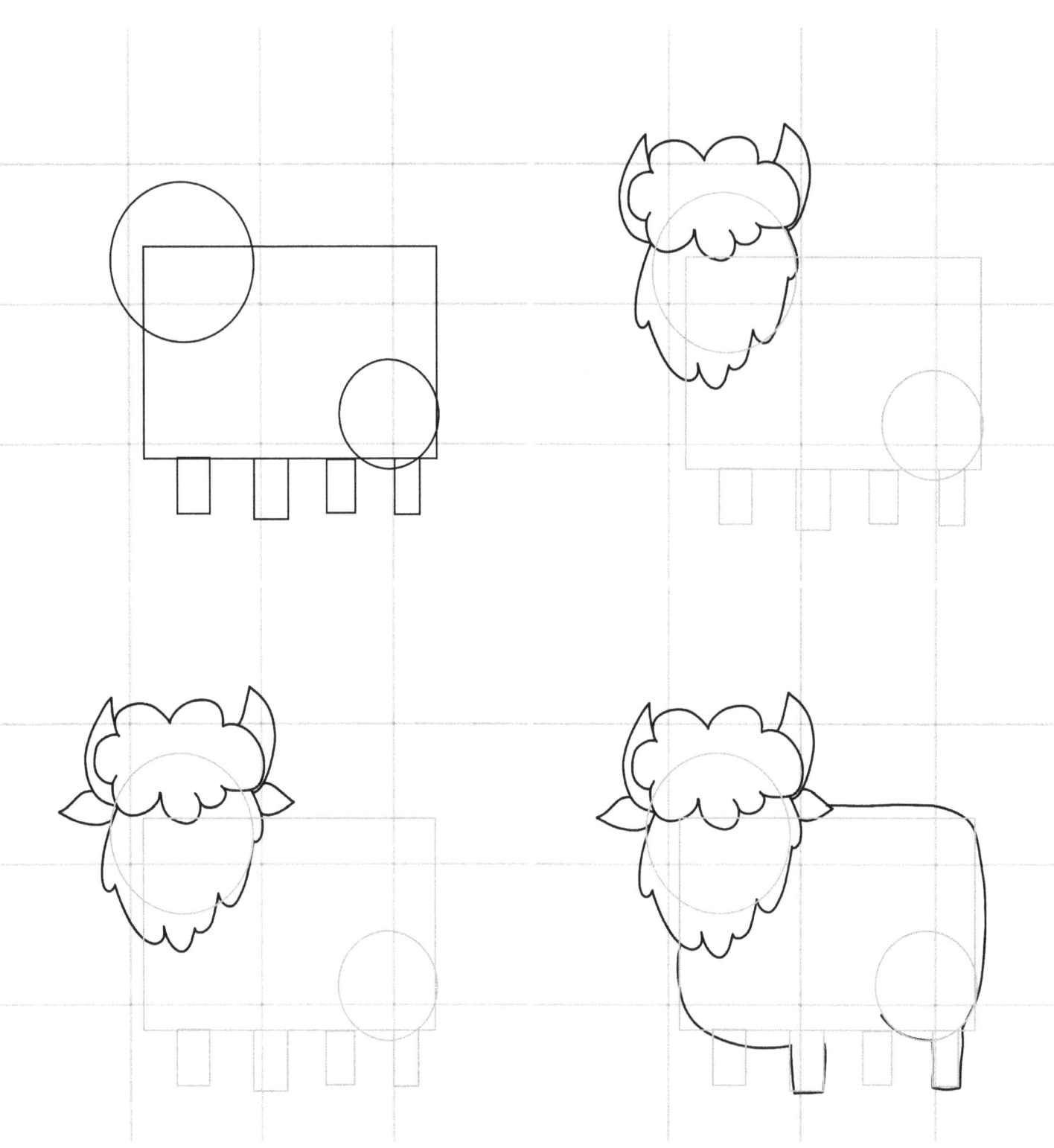

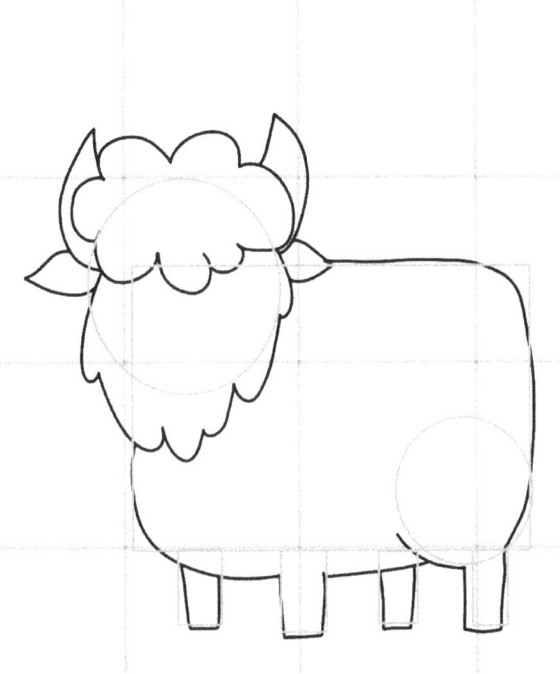
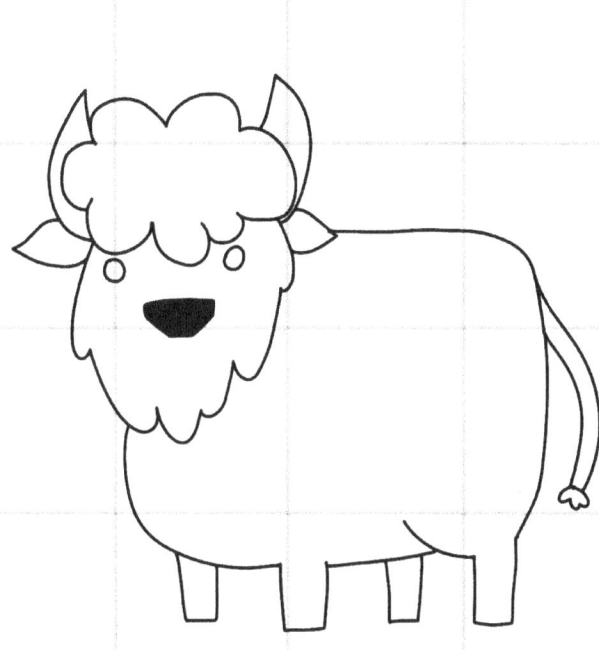

TRY it HERE!

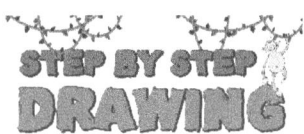

Bison

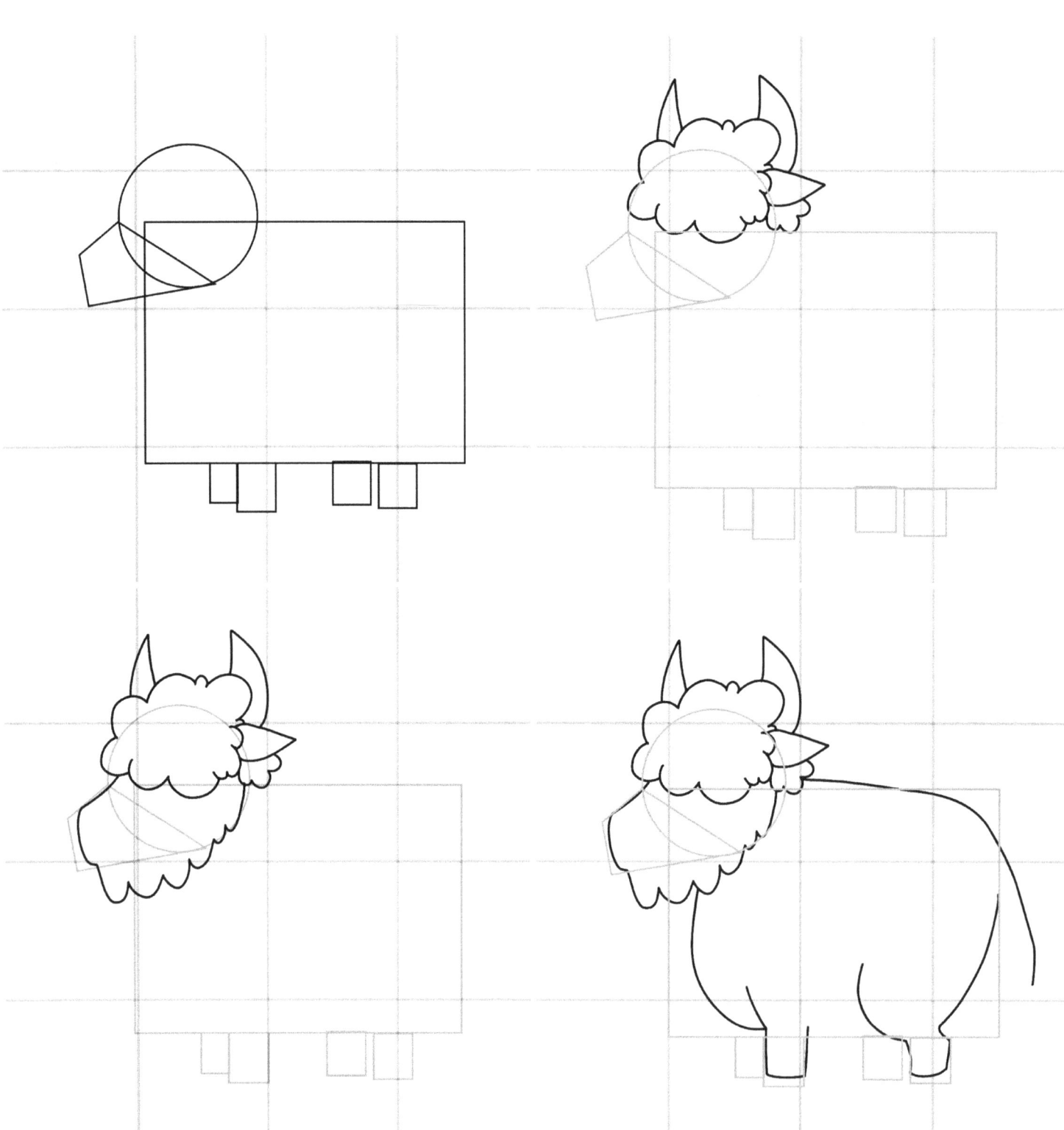

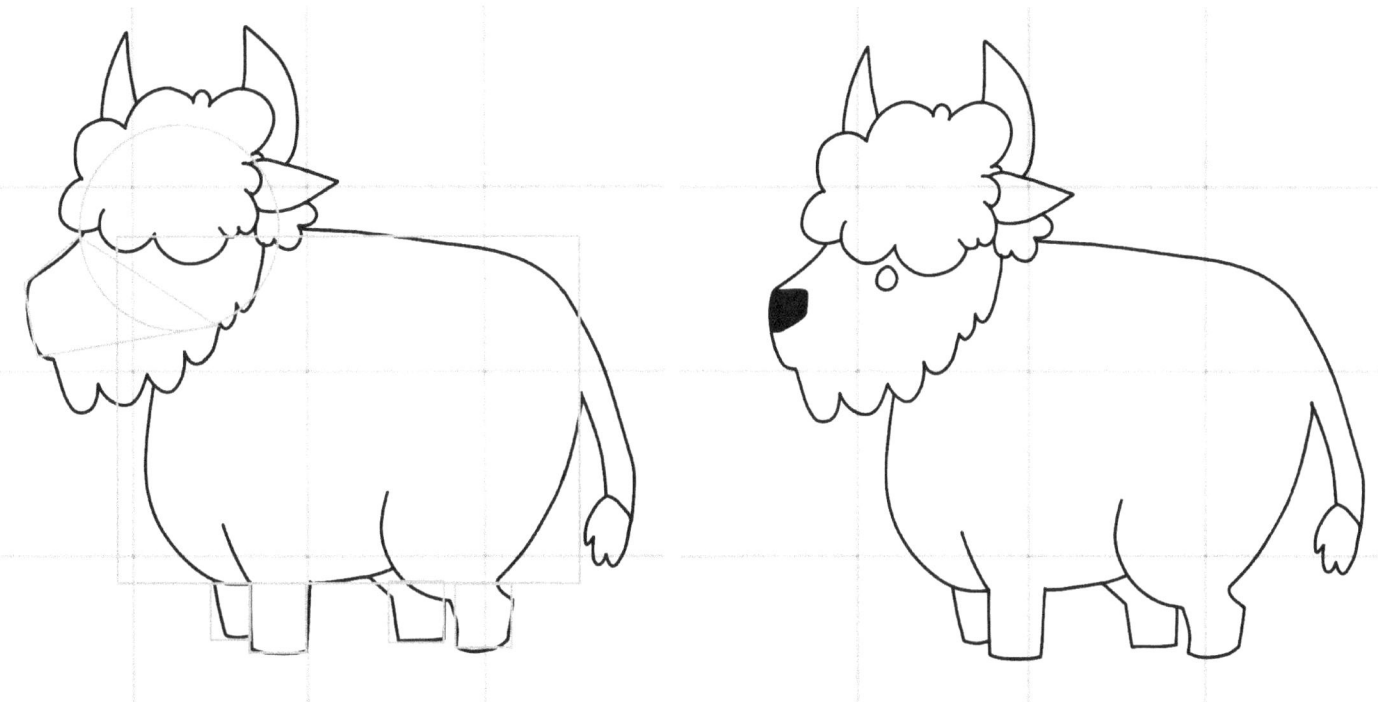

TRY it HERE!

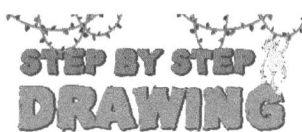

CHEETAH

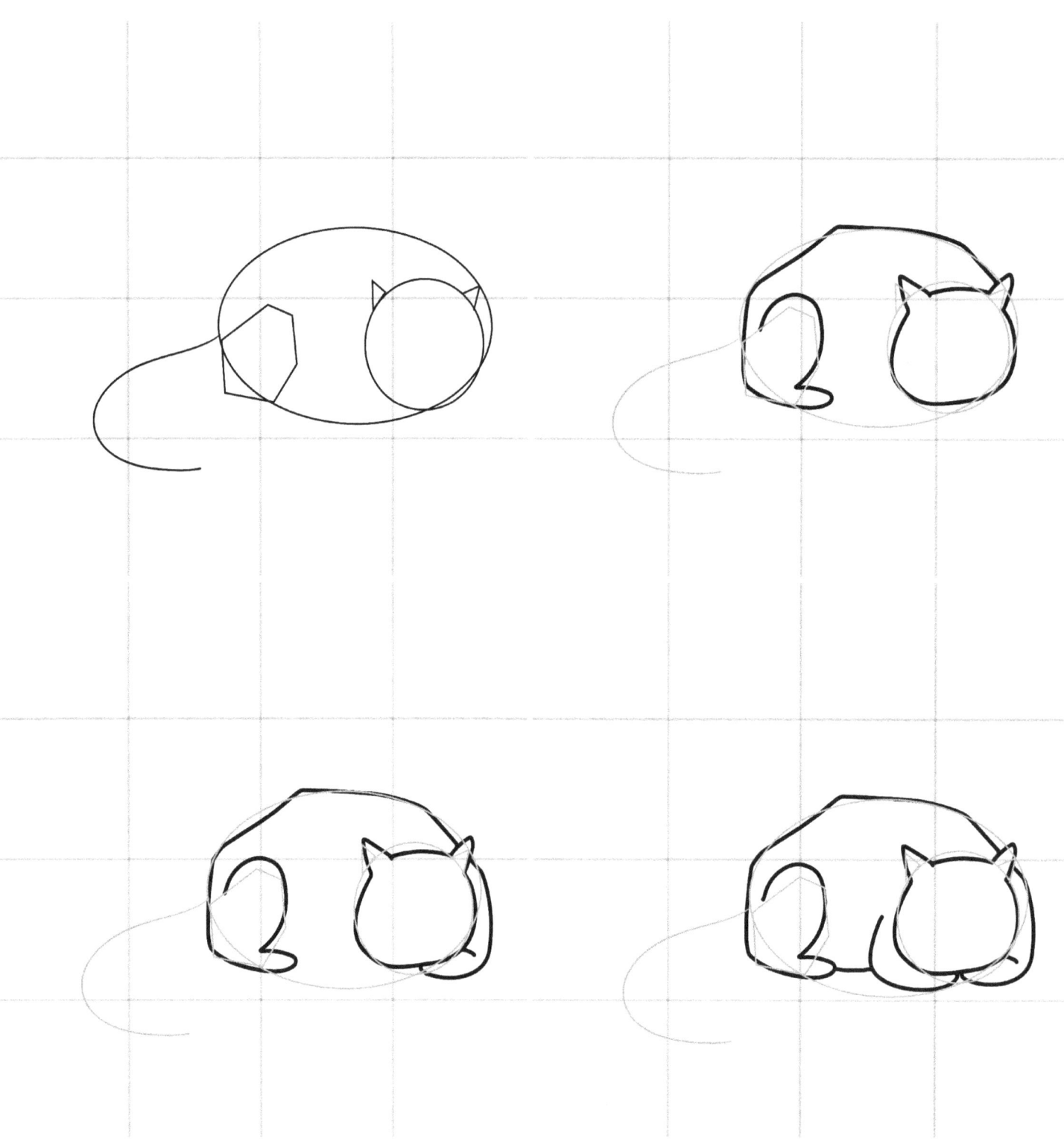

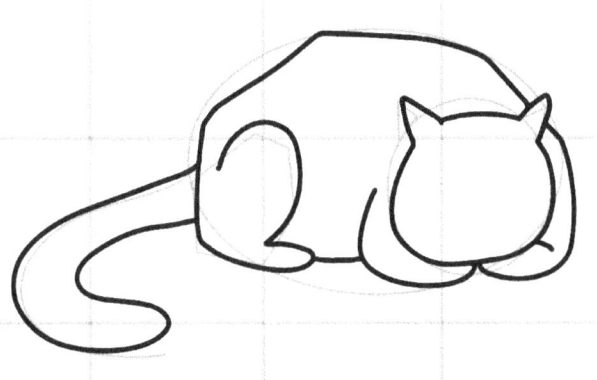 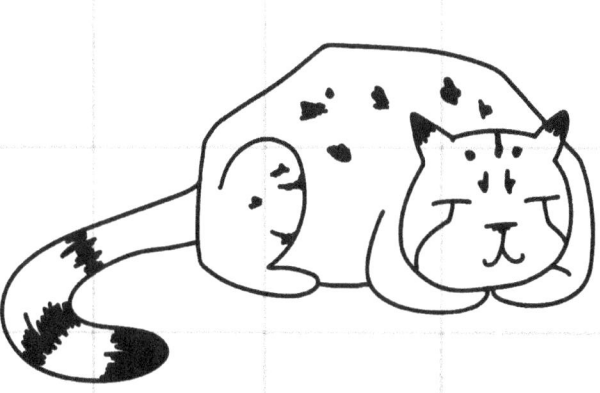

TRY it HERE!

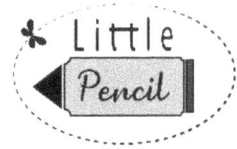 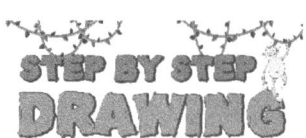

CHEETAH

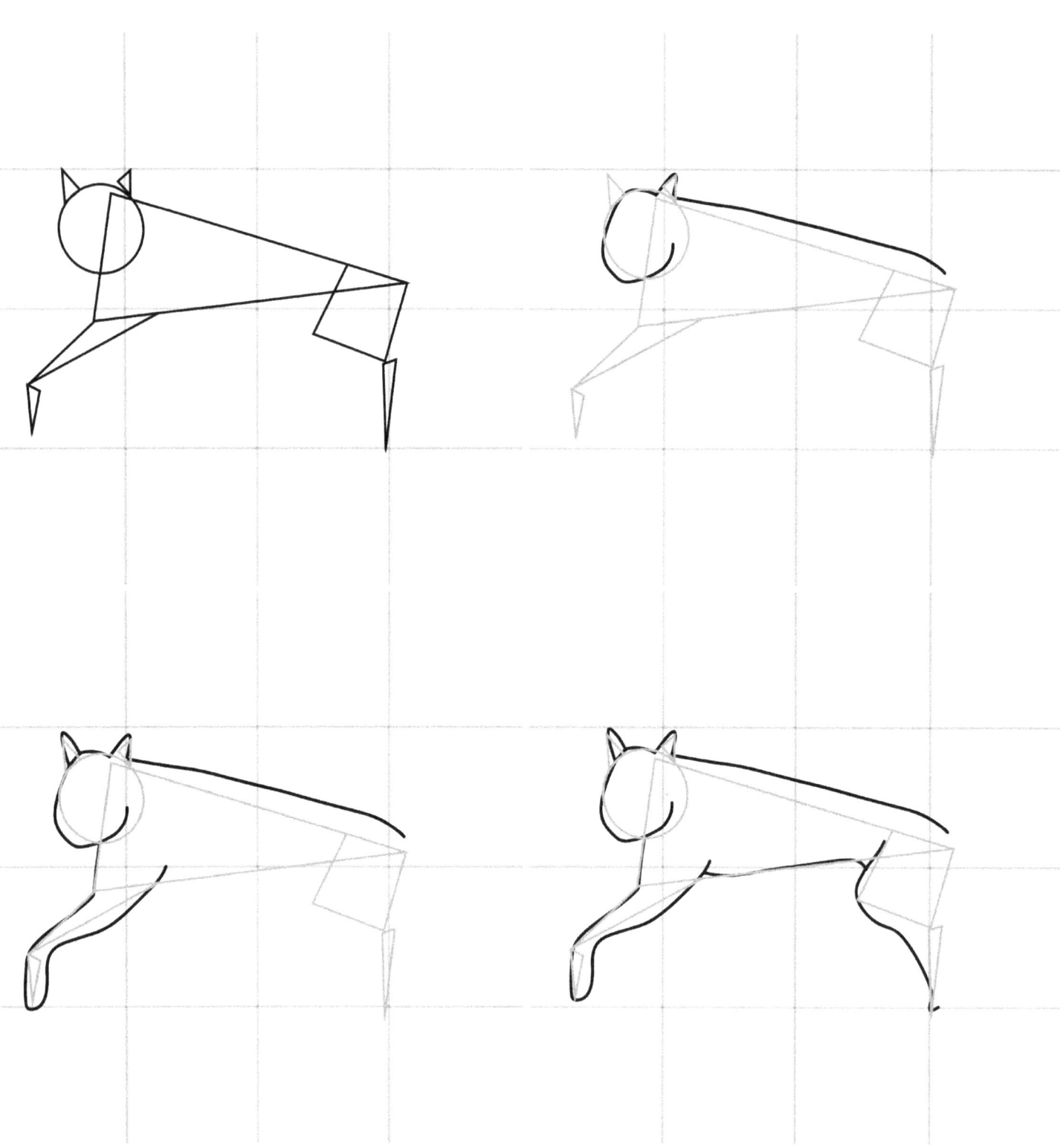

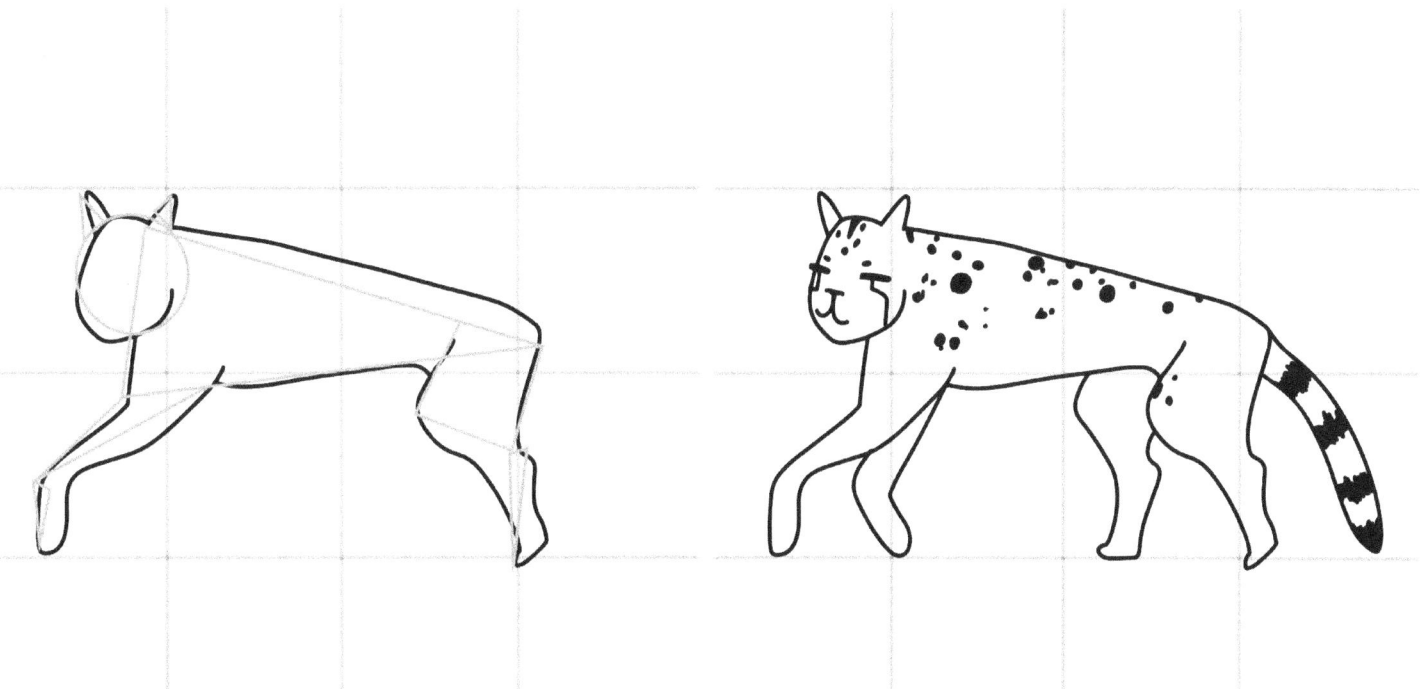

TRY iT HERE!

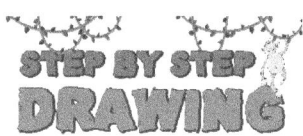

DOLPHIN

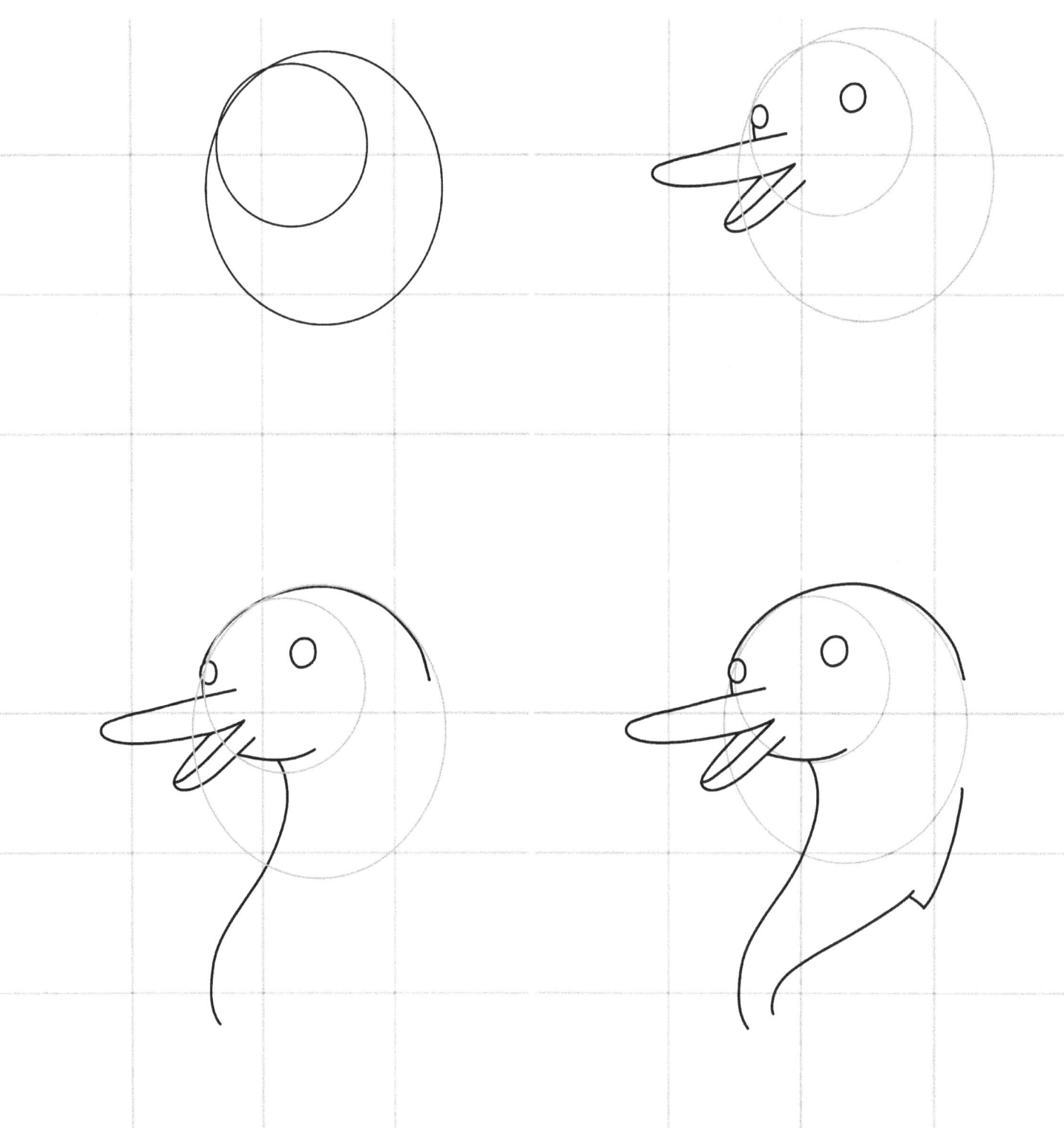

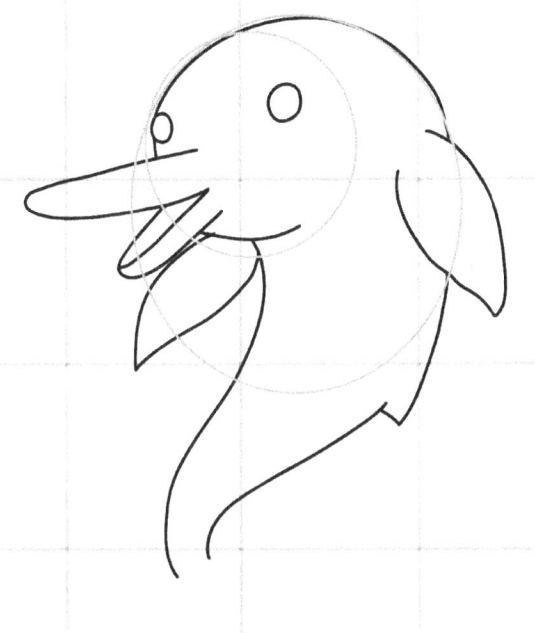
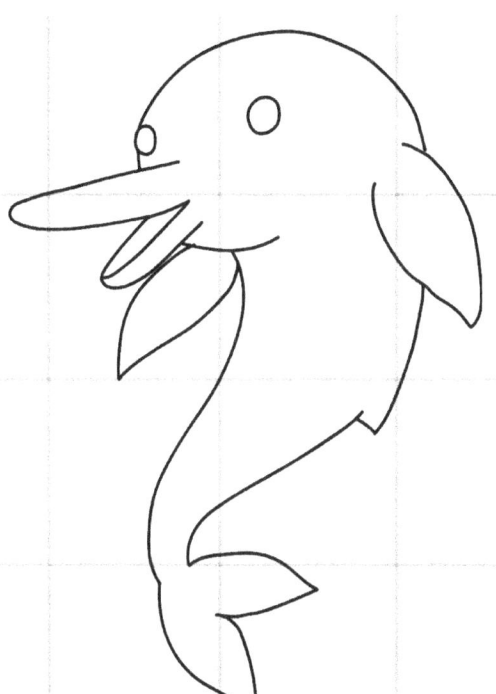

TRY it HERE!

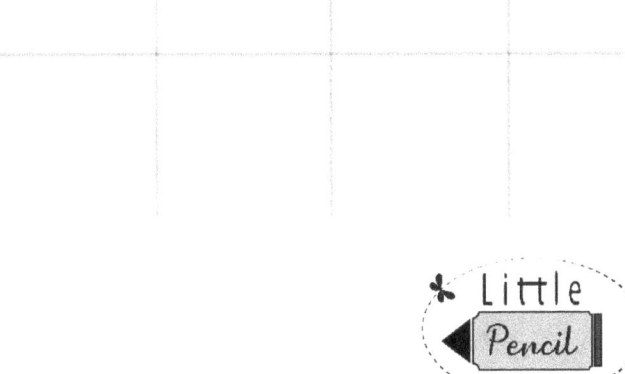
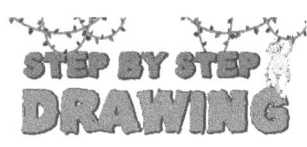

DOLPHIN

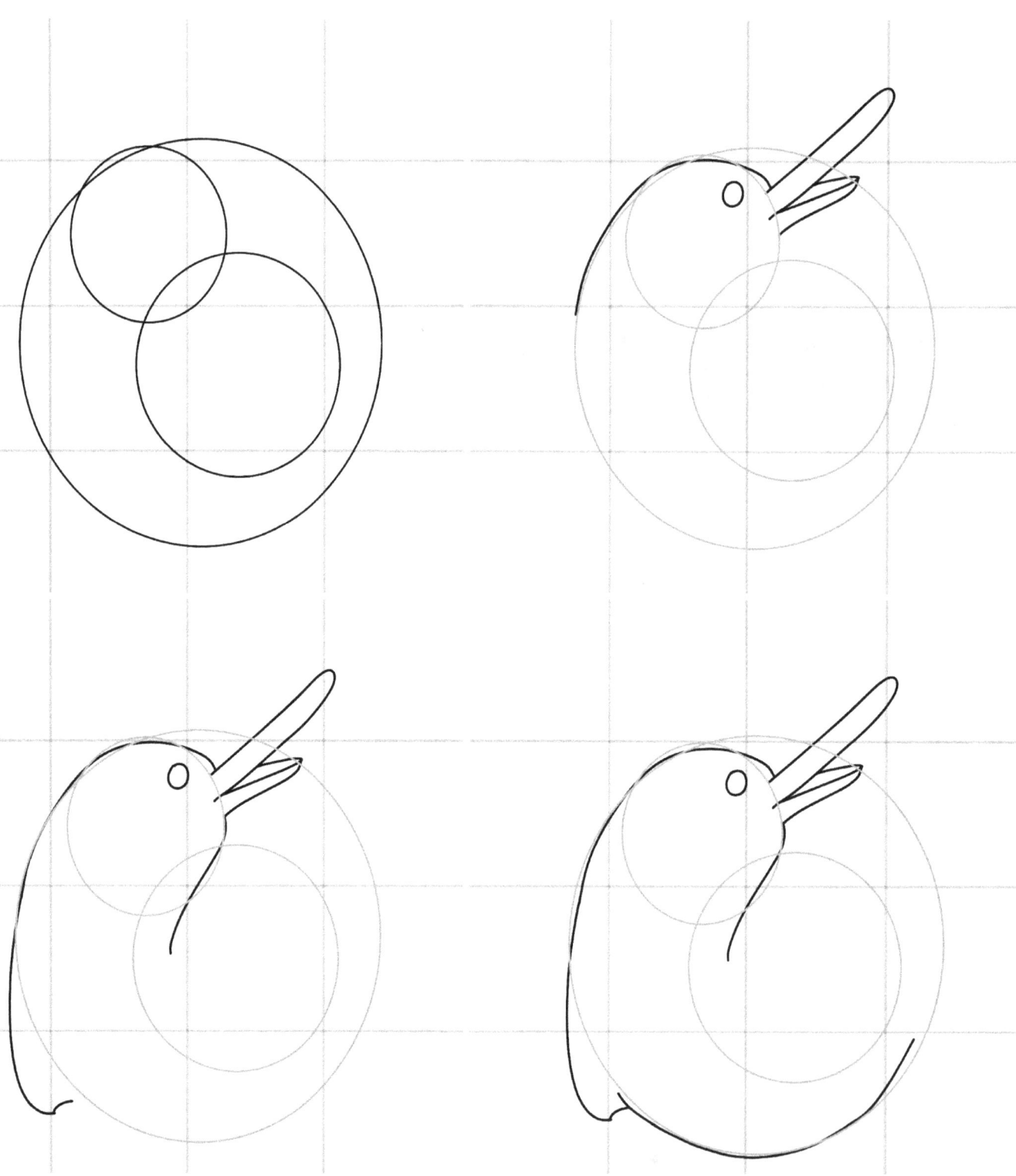

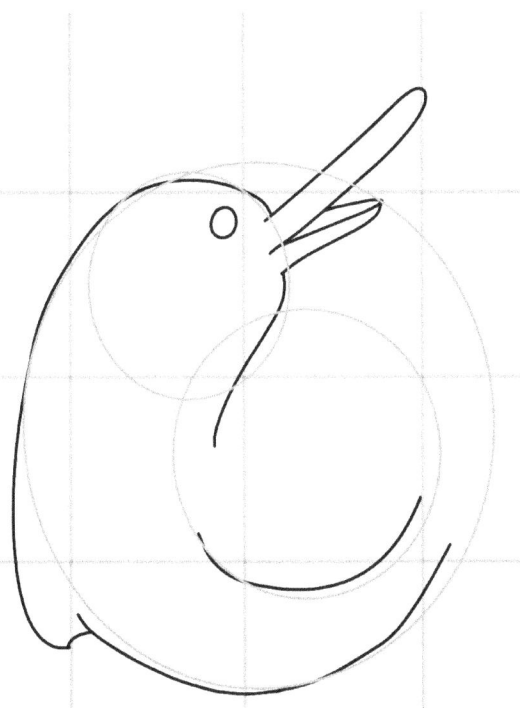

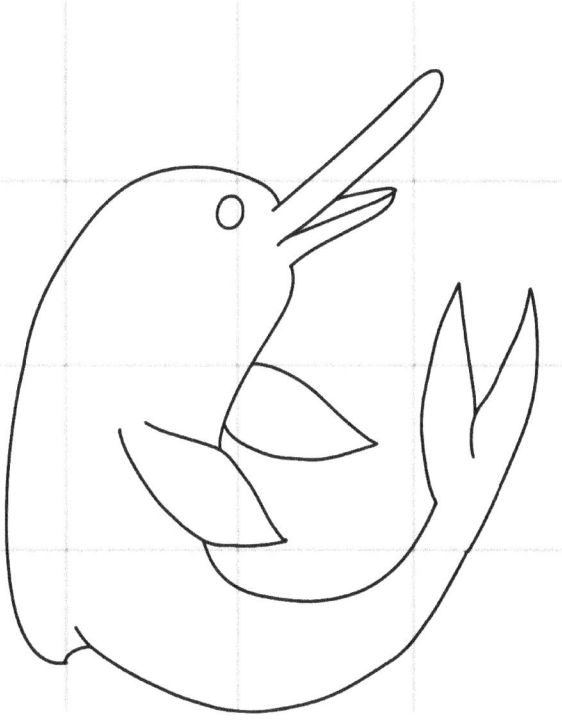

TRY it HERE!

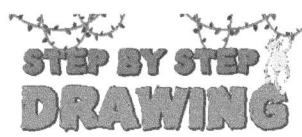

ELEPHANT

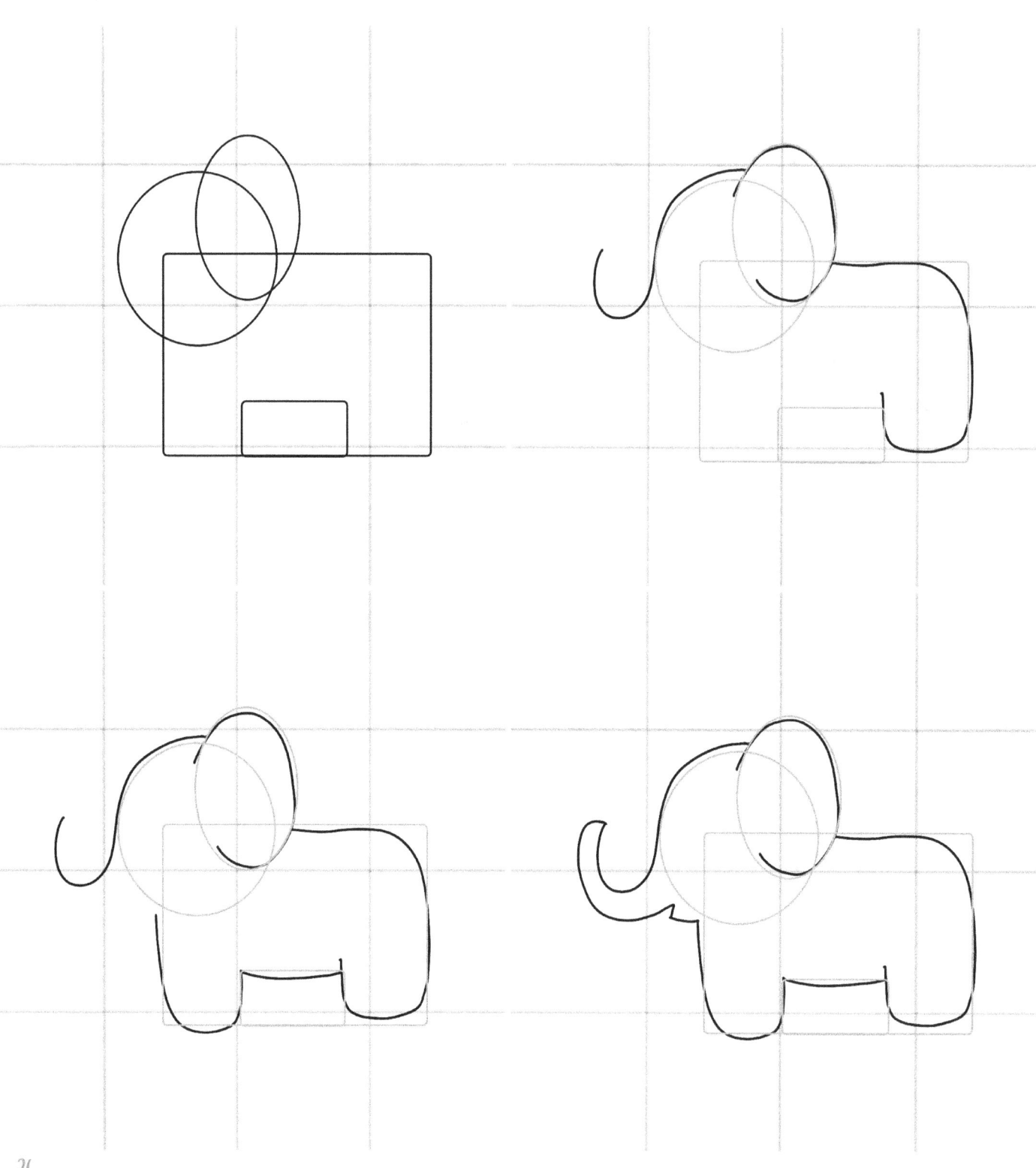

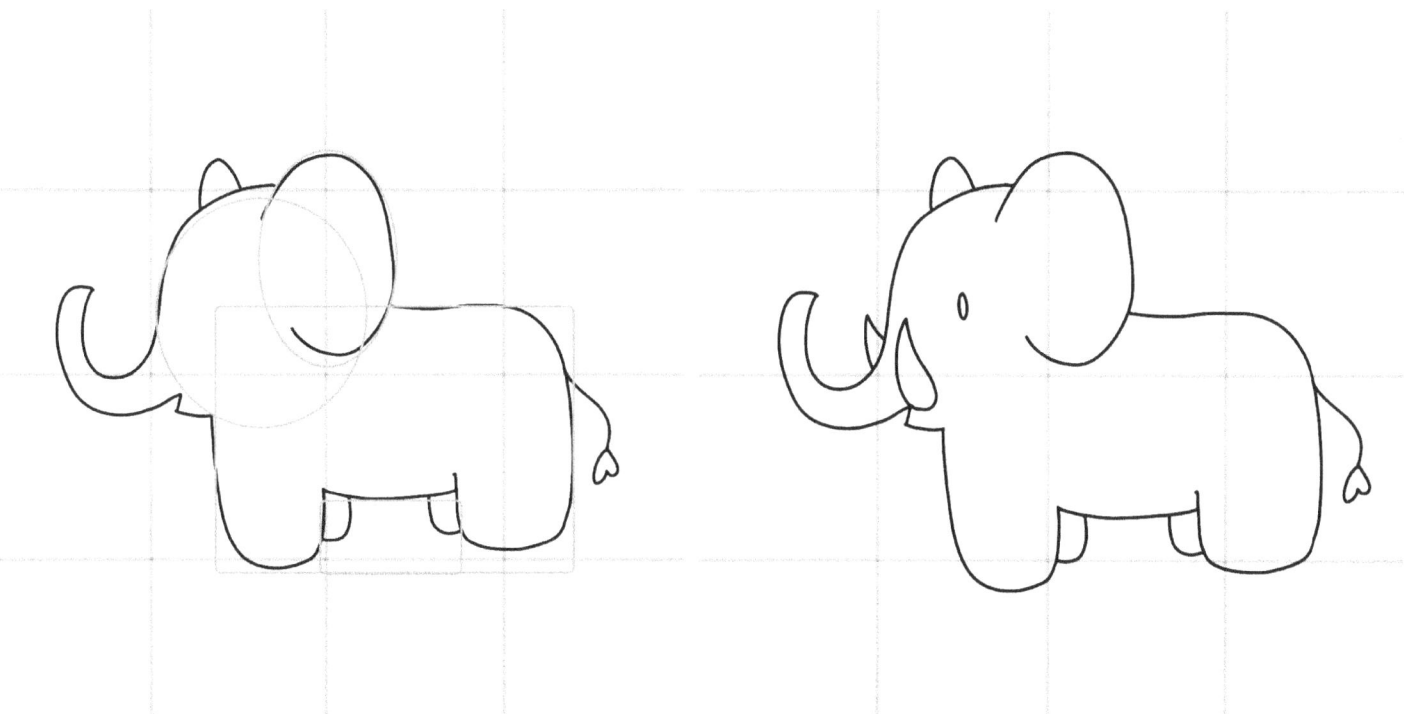

TRY it HERE!

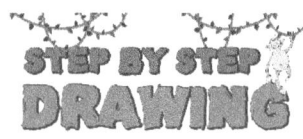

ELEPHANT

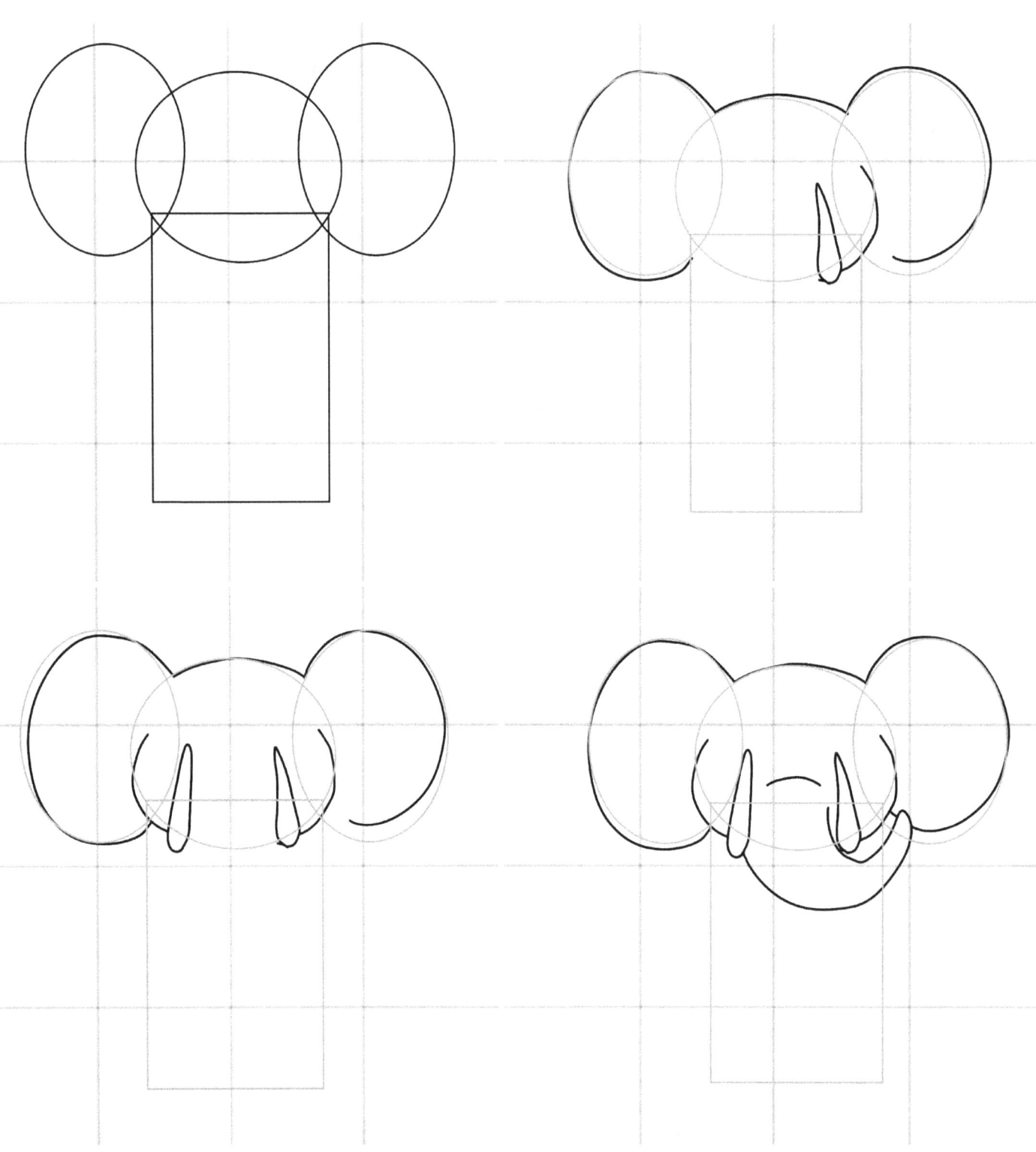

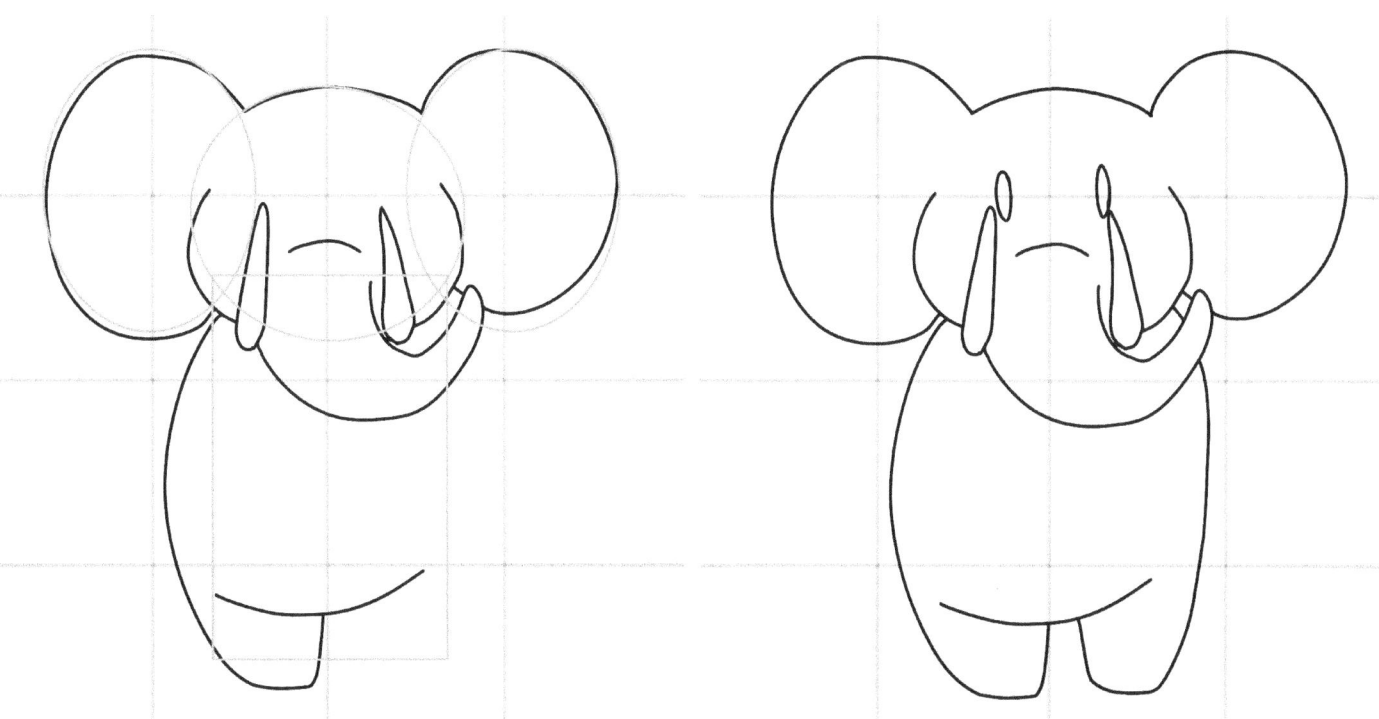

TRY IT HERE!

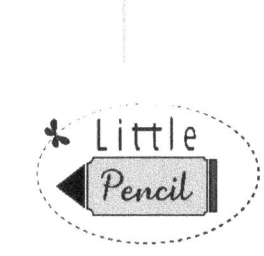
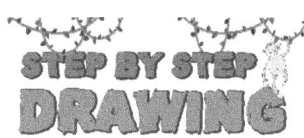

FLAMINGO

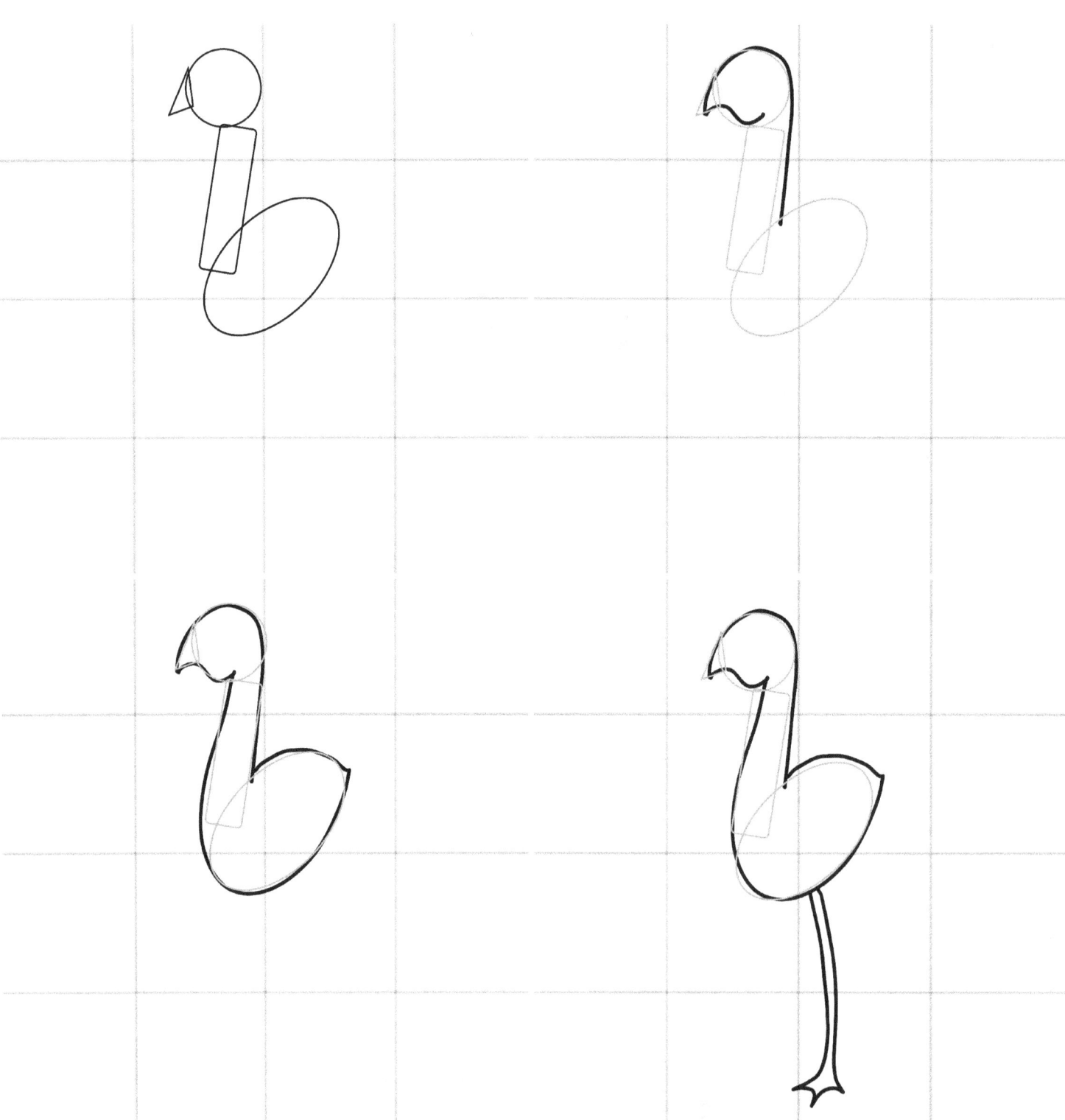

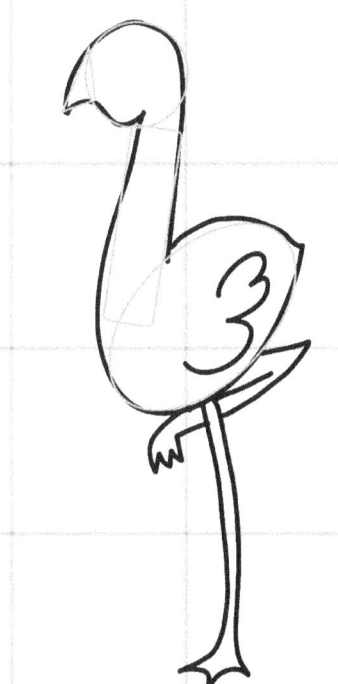

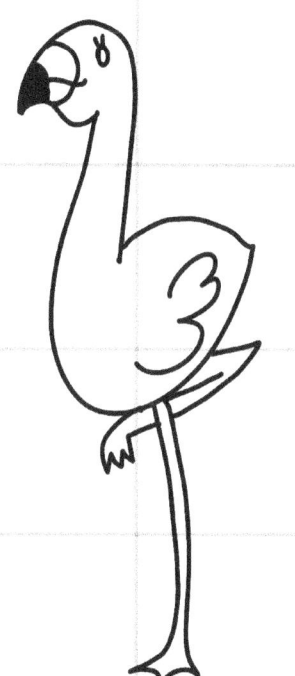

TRY it HERE!

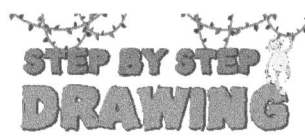

FLAMINGO

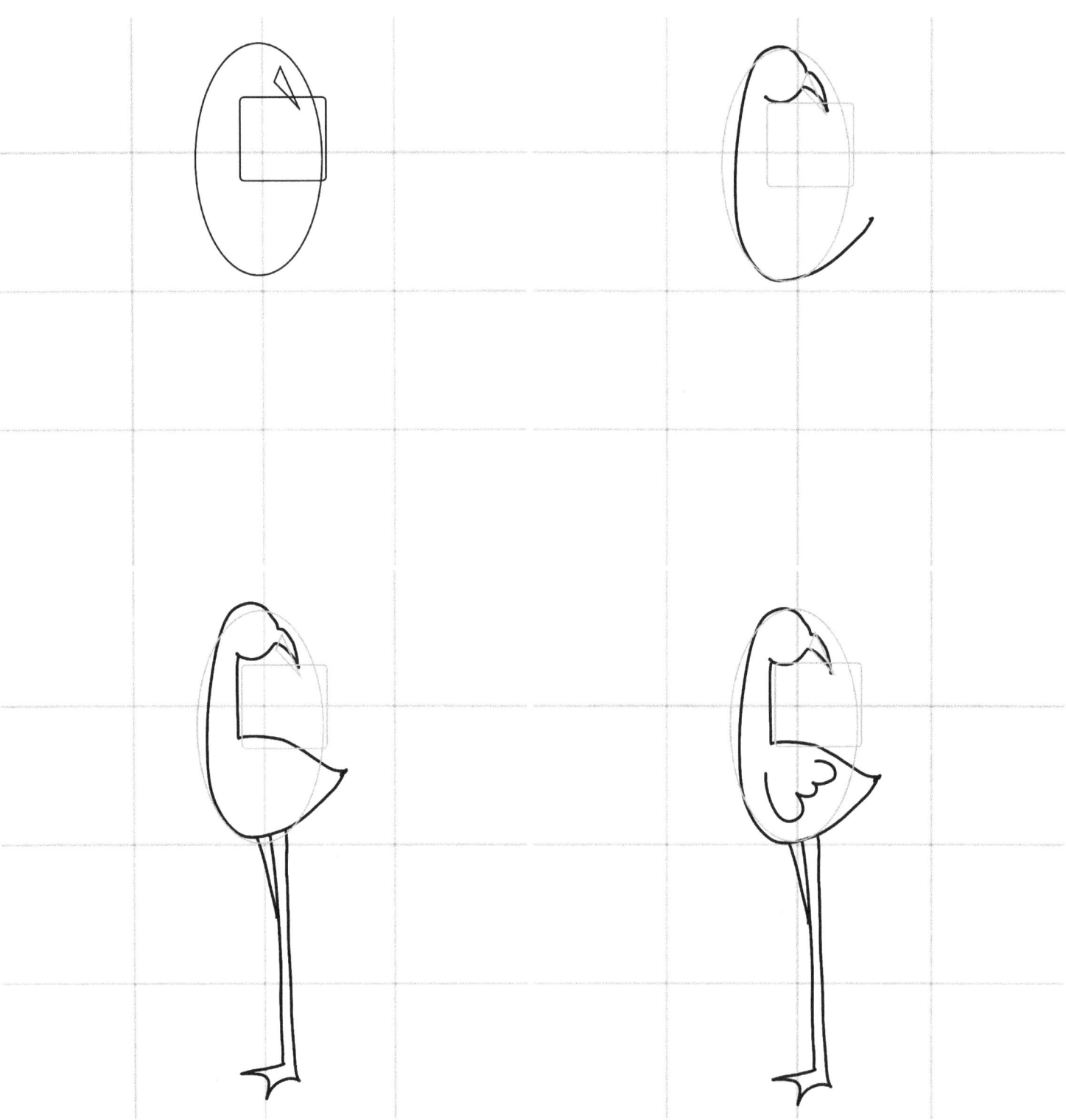

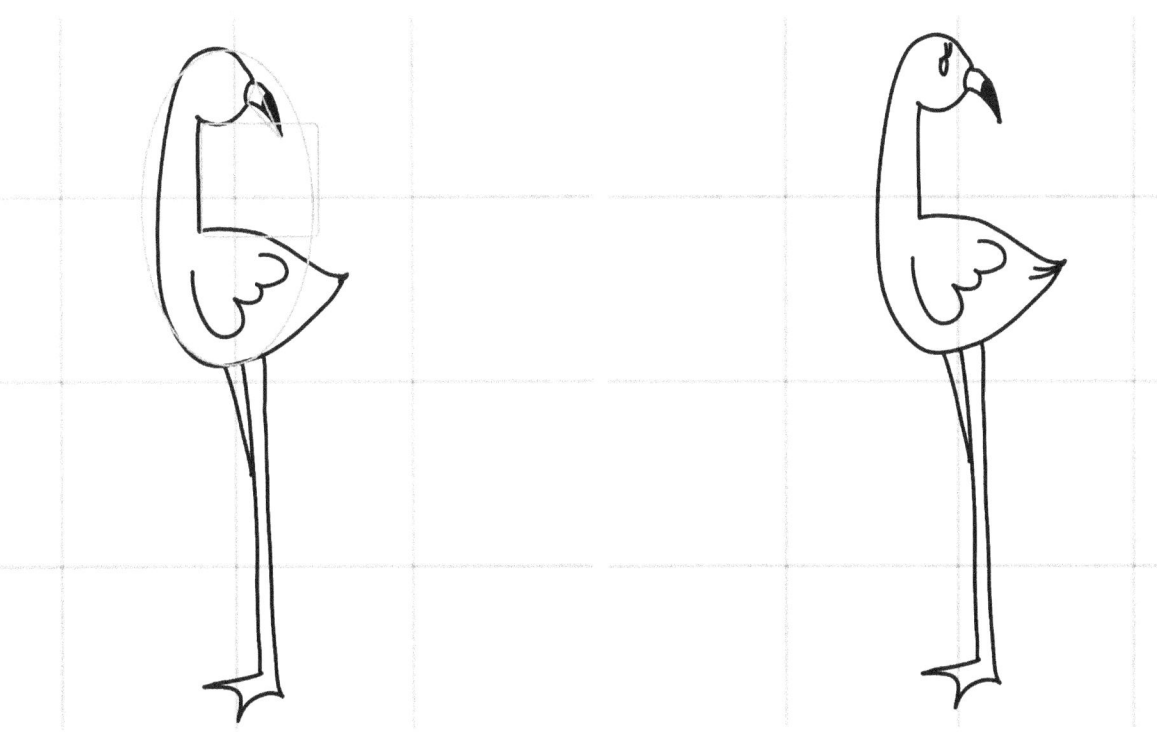

TRY it HERE!

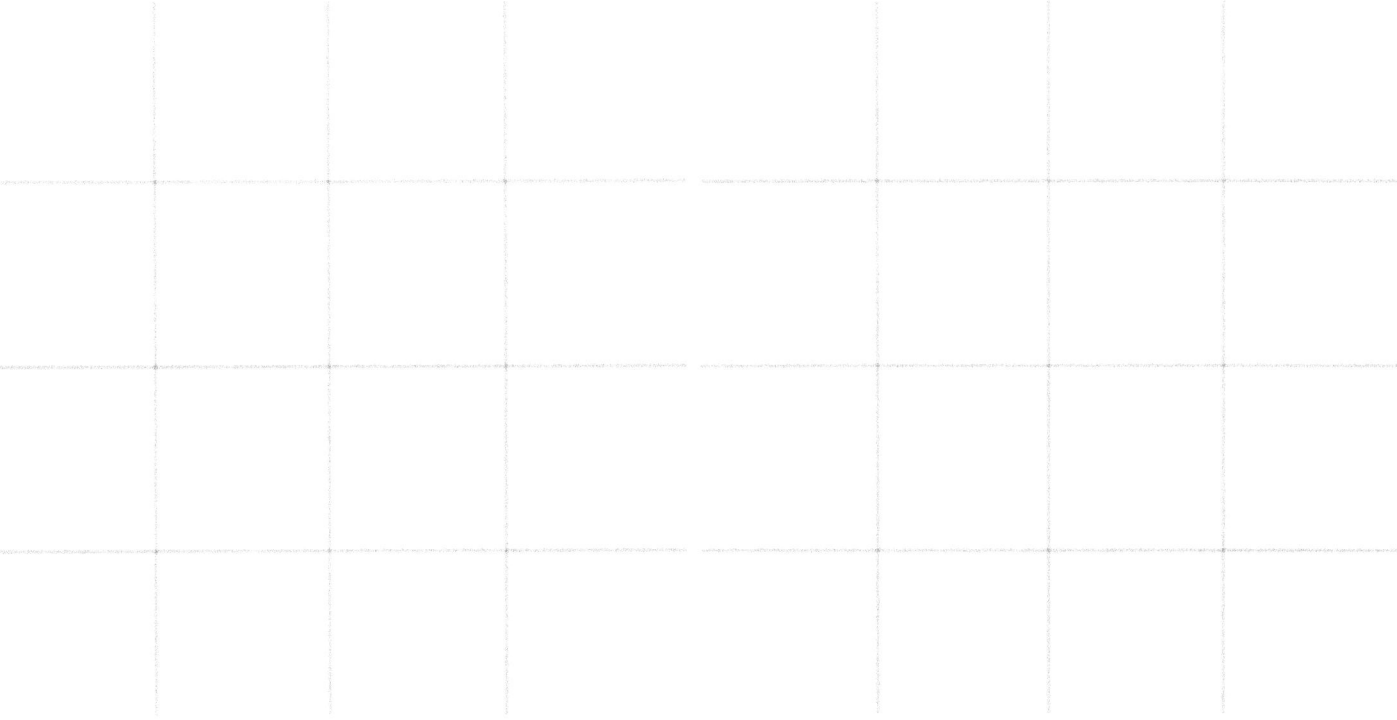

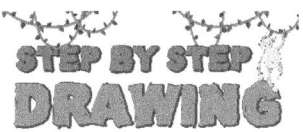

GIANT ANTEATER

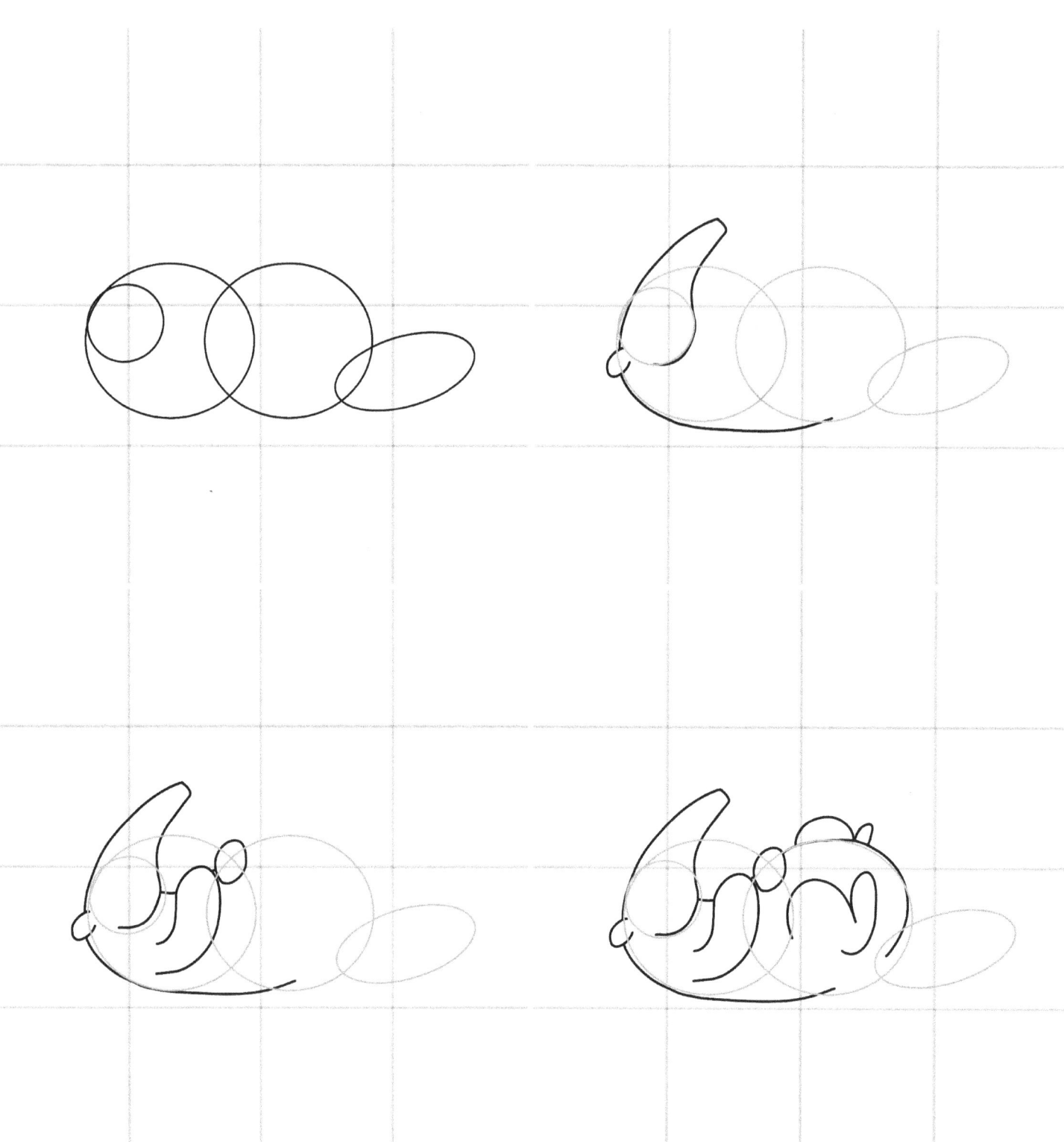

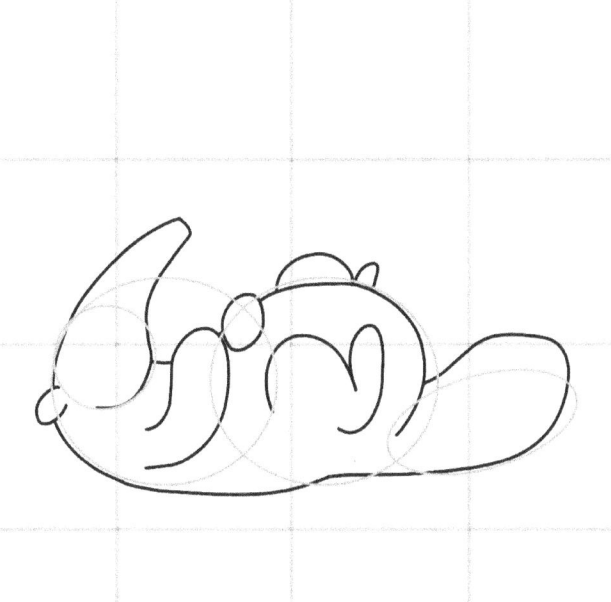 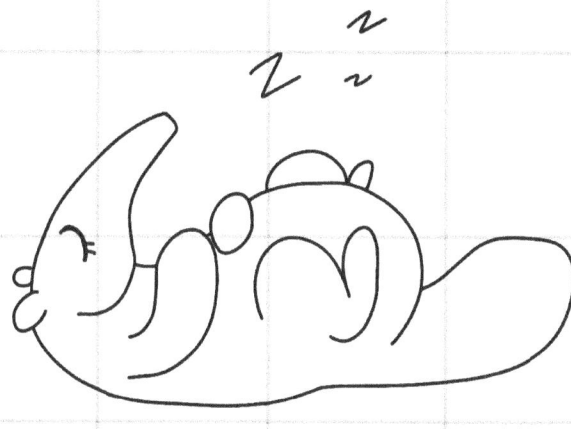

TRY iT HERE!

 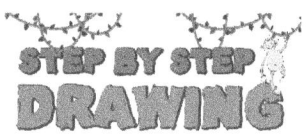

GIANT ANTEATER

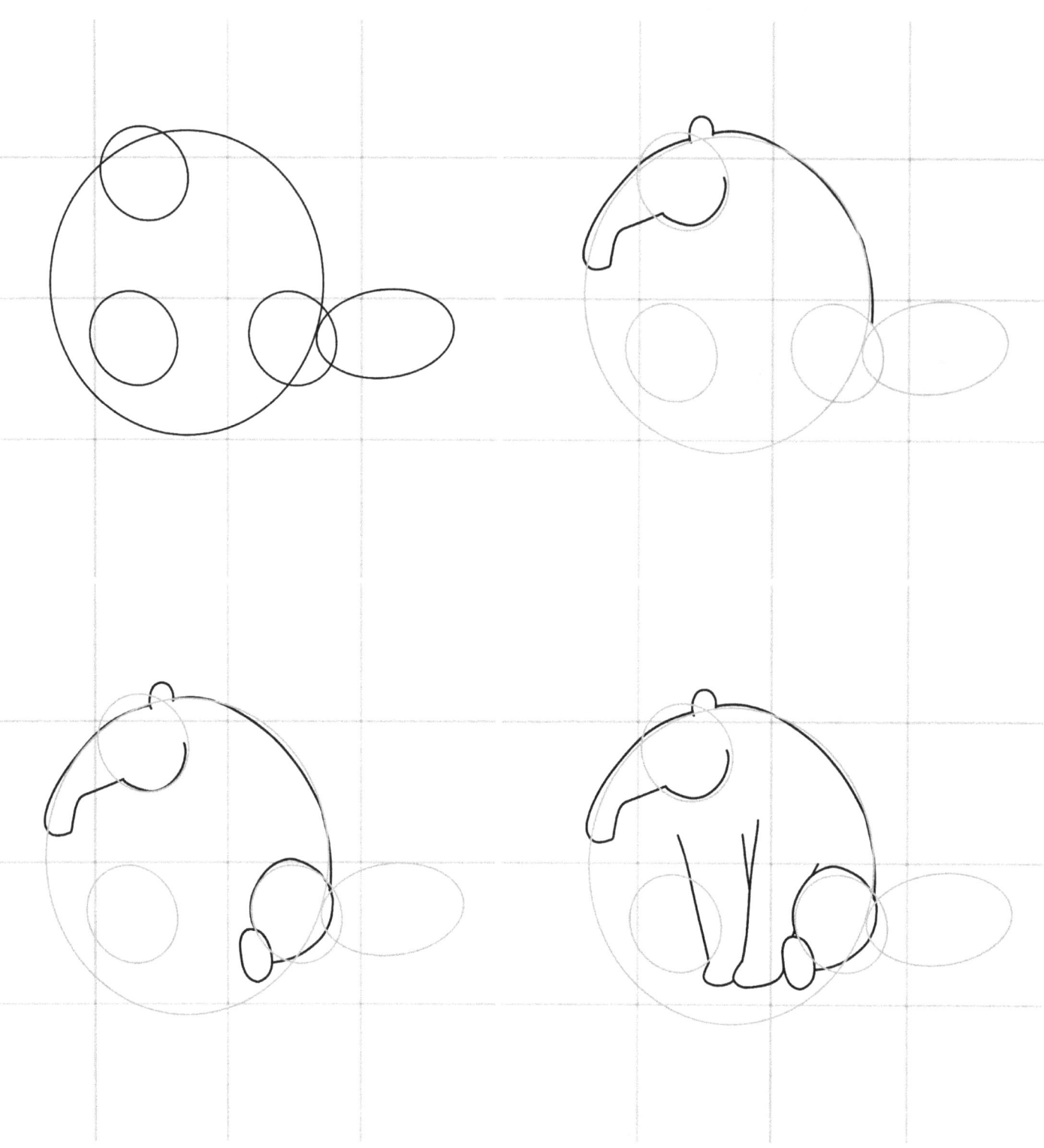

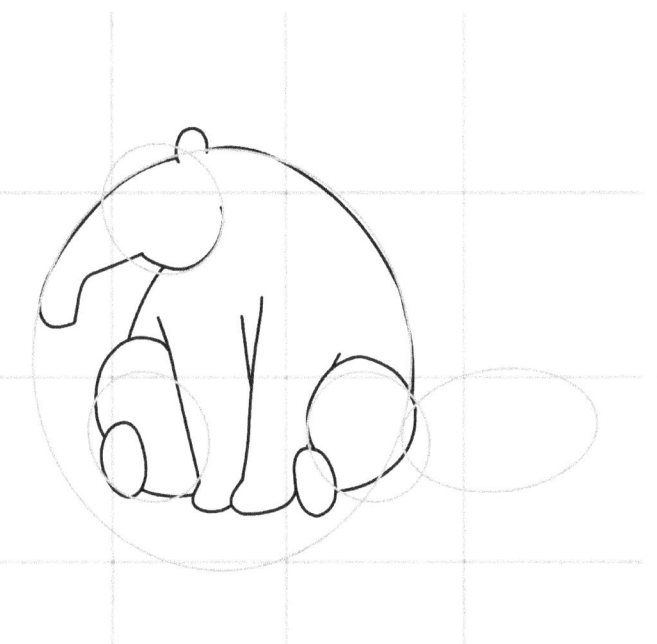
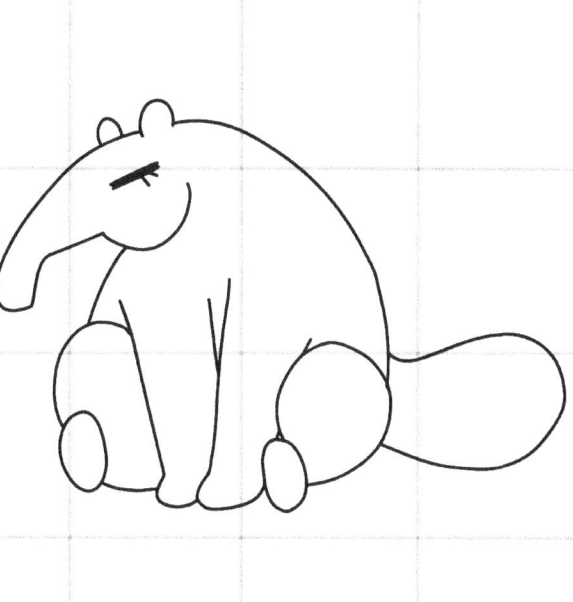

TRY it HERE!

 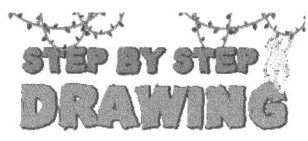

GIRAFFE

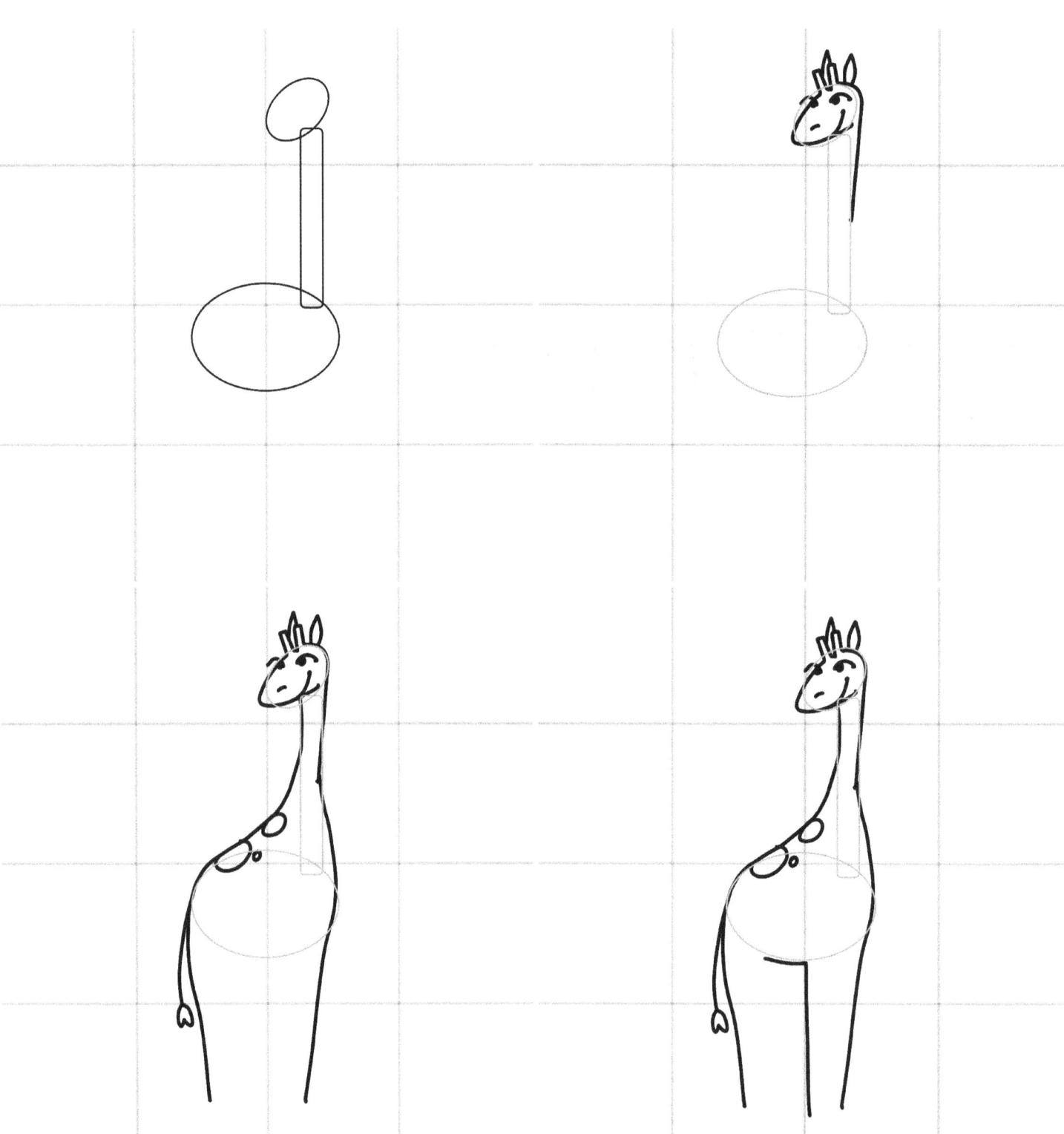

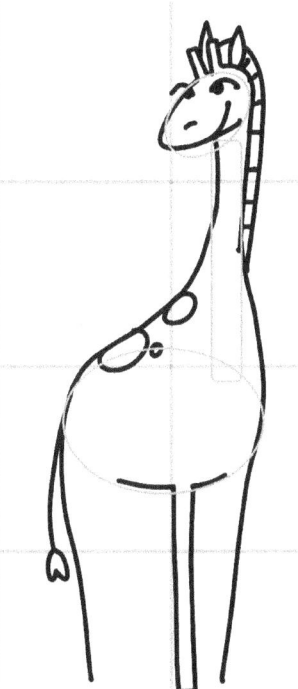

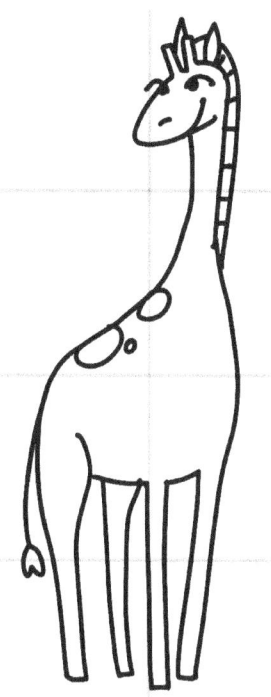

TRY it HERE!

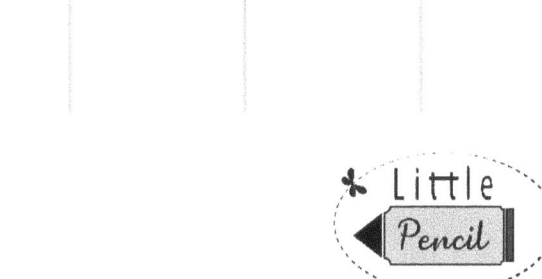

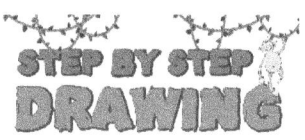

GORILLA

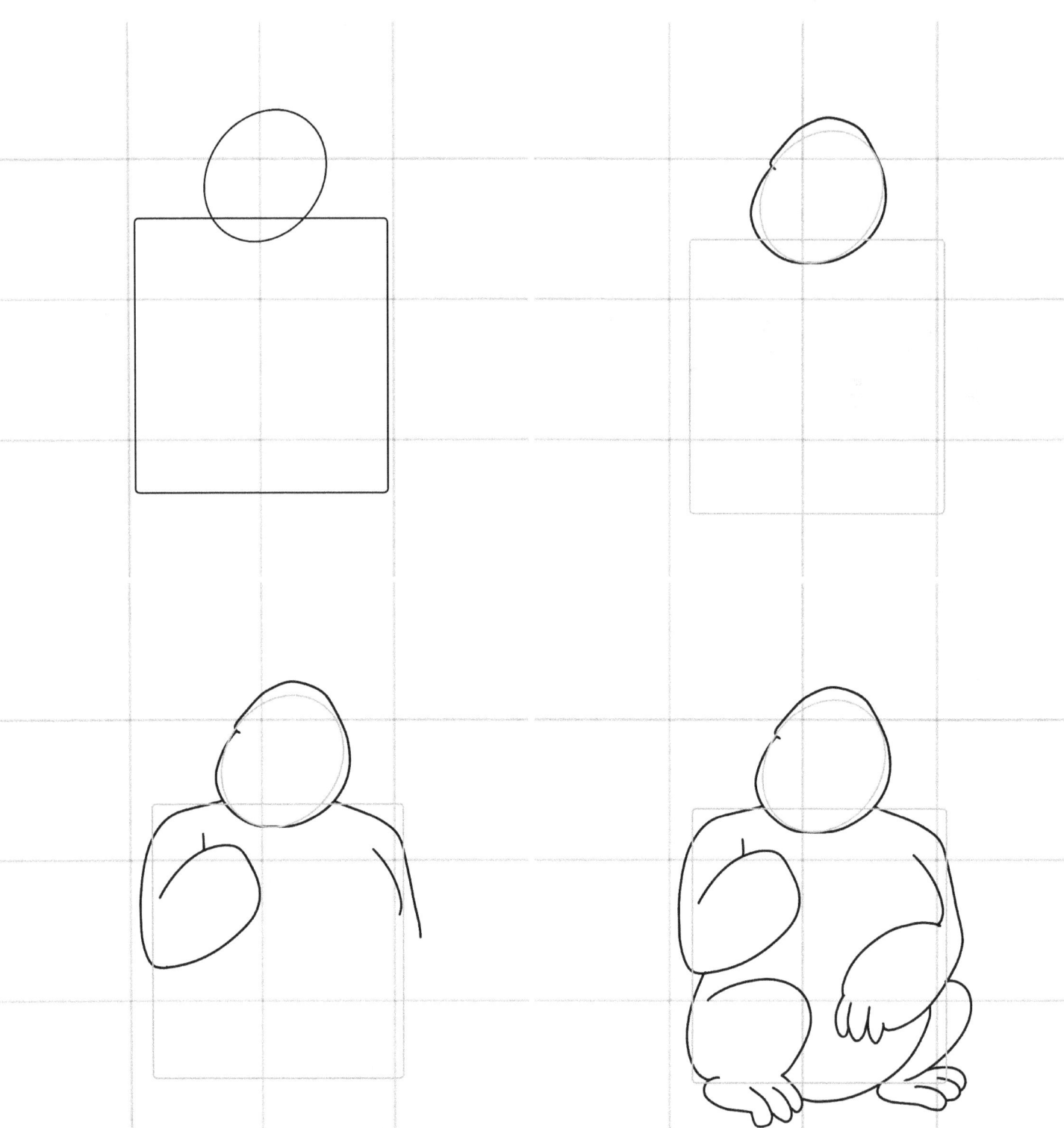

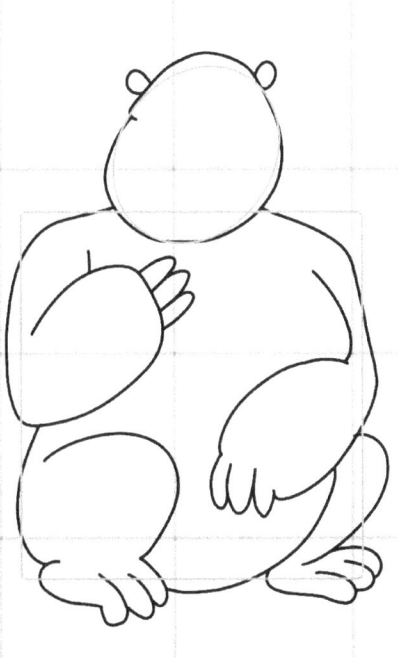

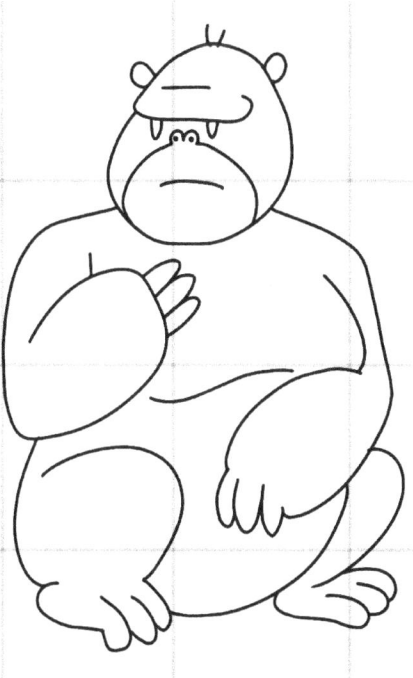

TRY iT HERE!

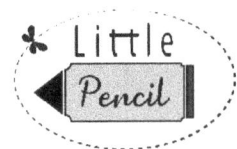
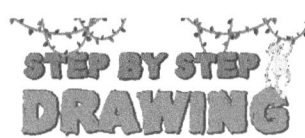

GORILLA

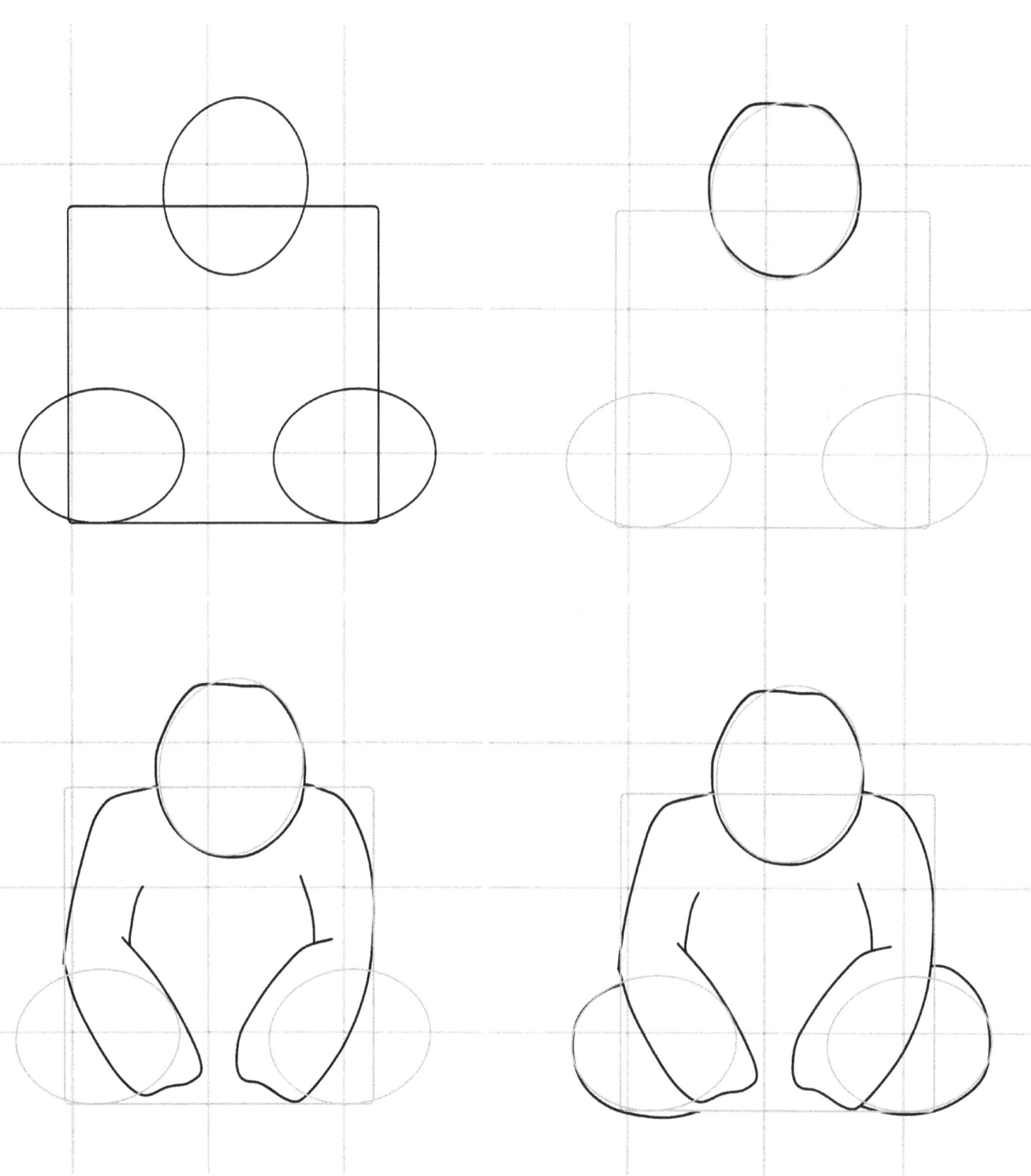

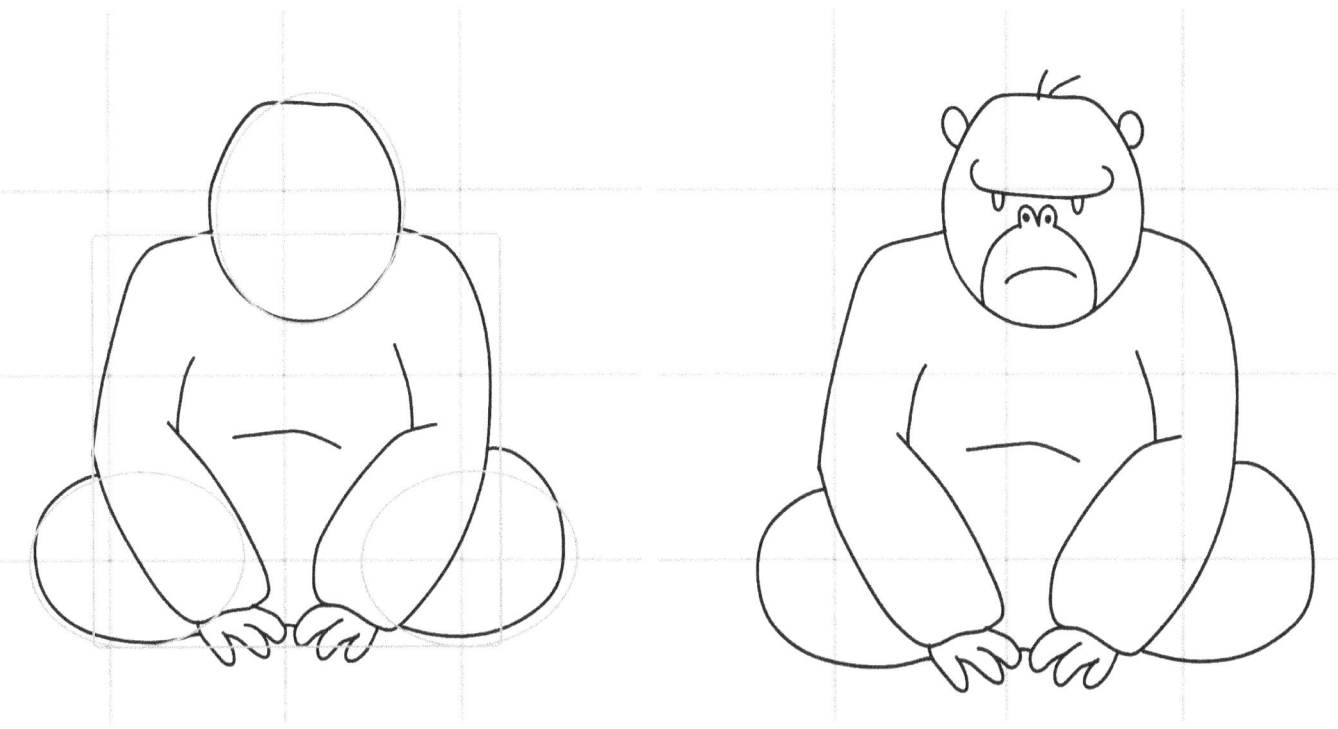

TRY iT HERE!

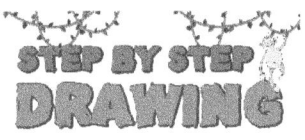

HARBOR SEAL

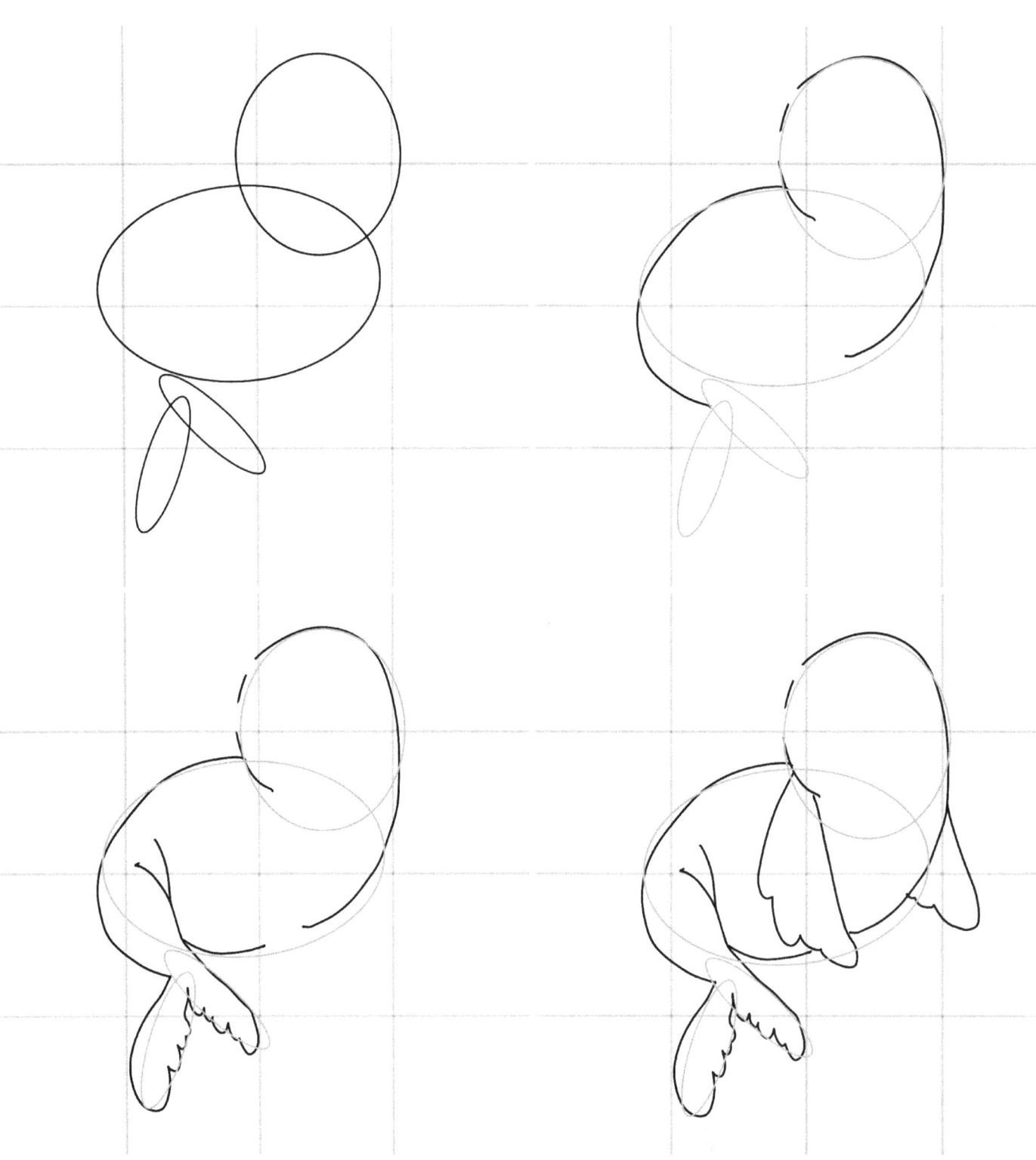

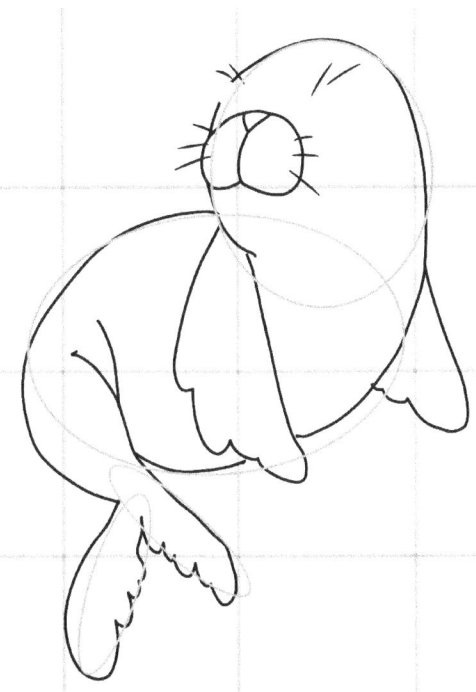

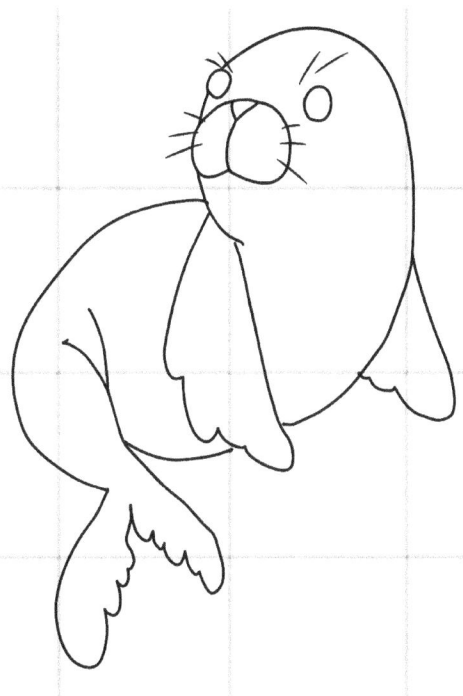

TRY it HERE!

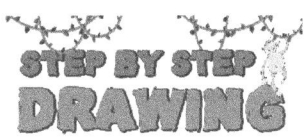

HARBOR SEAL

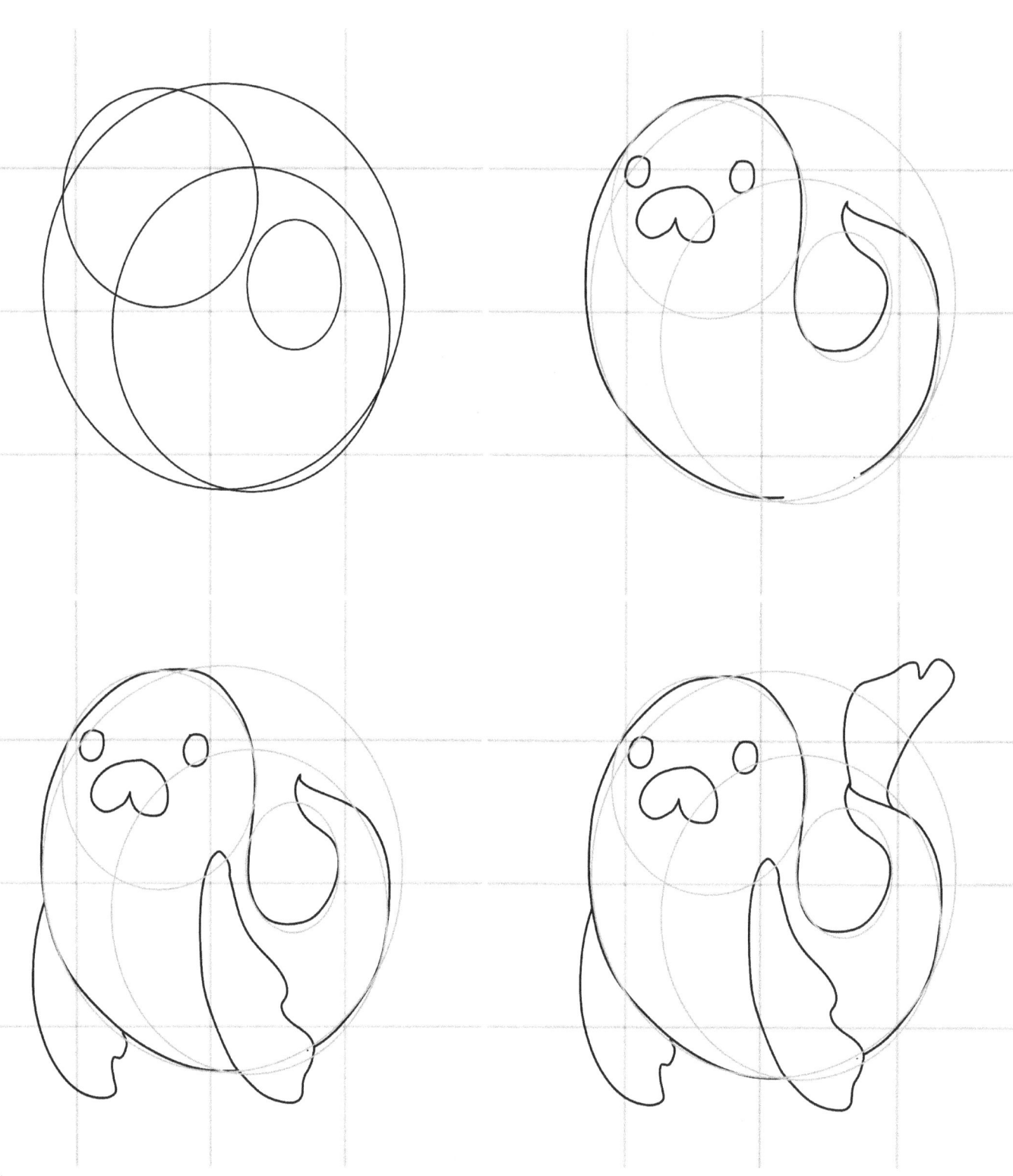

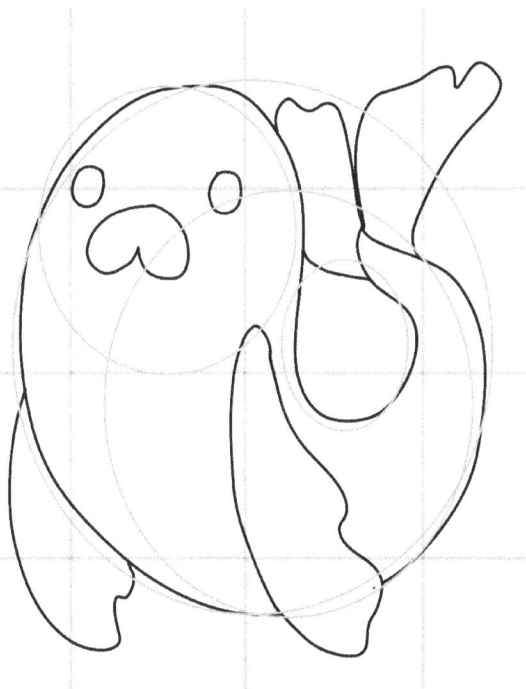
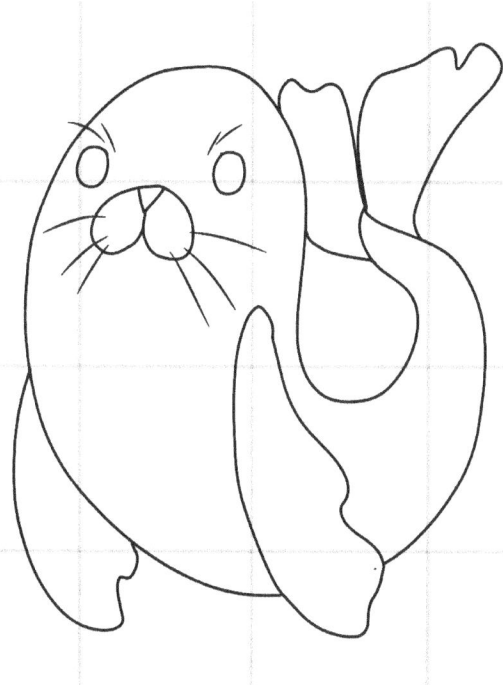

TRY iT HERE!

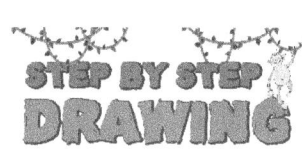

Hippo

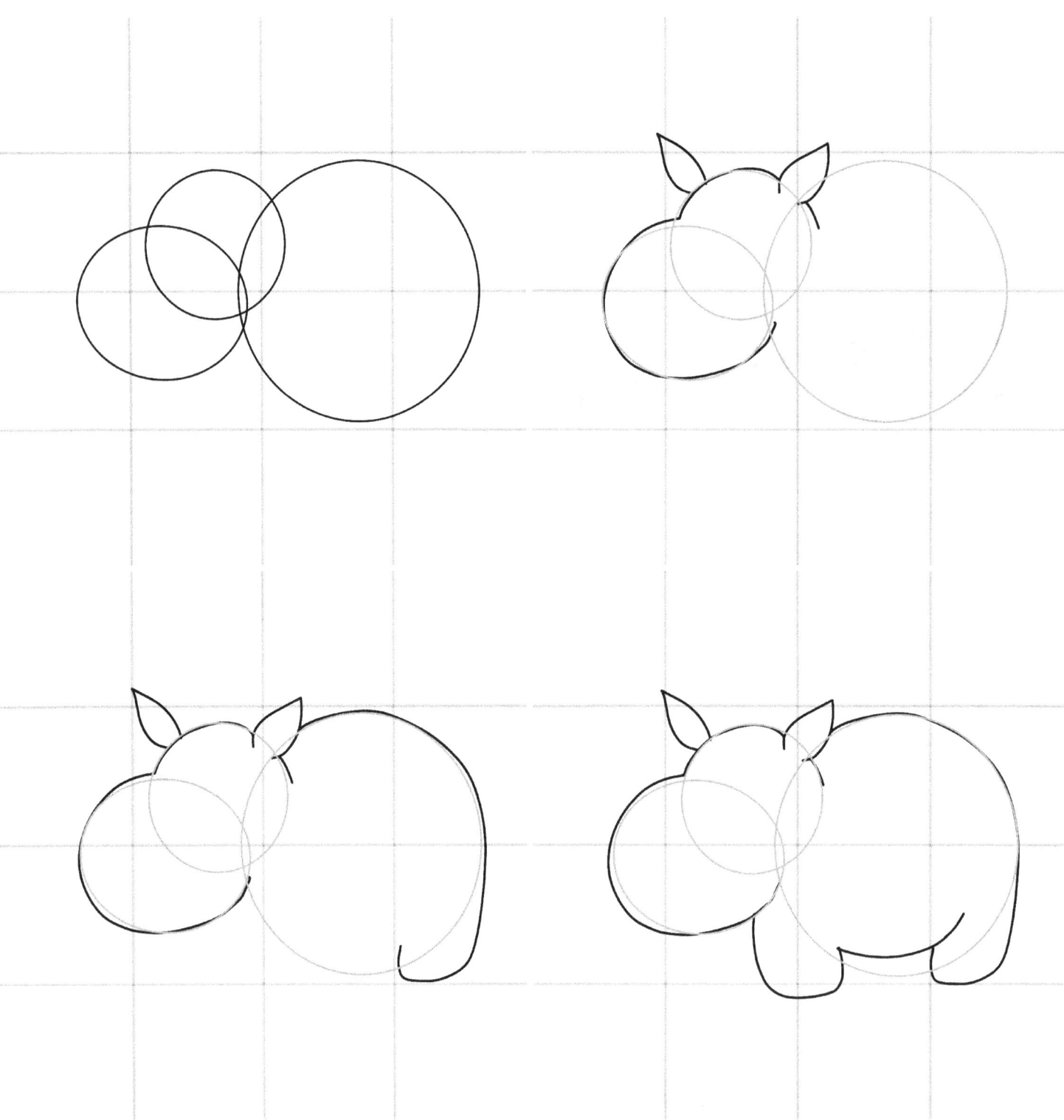

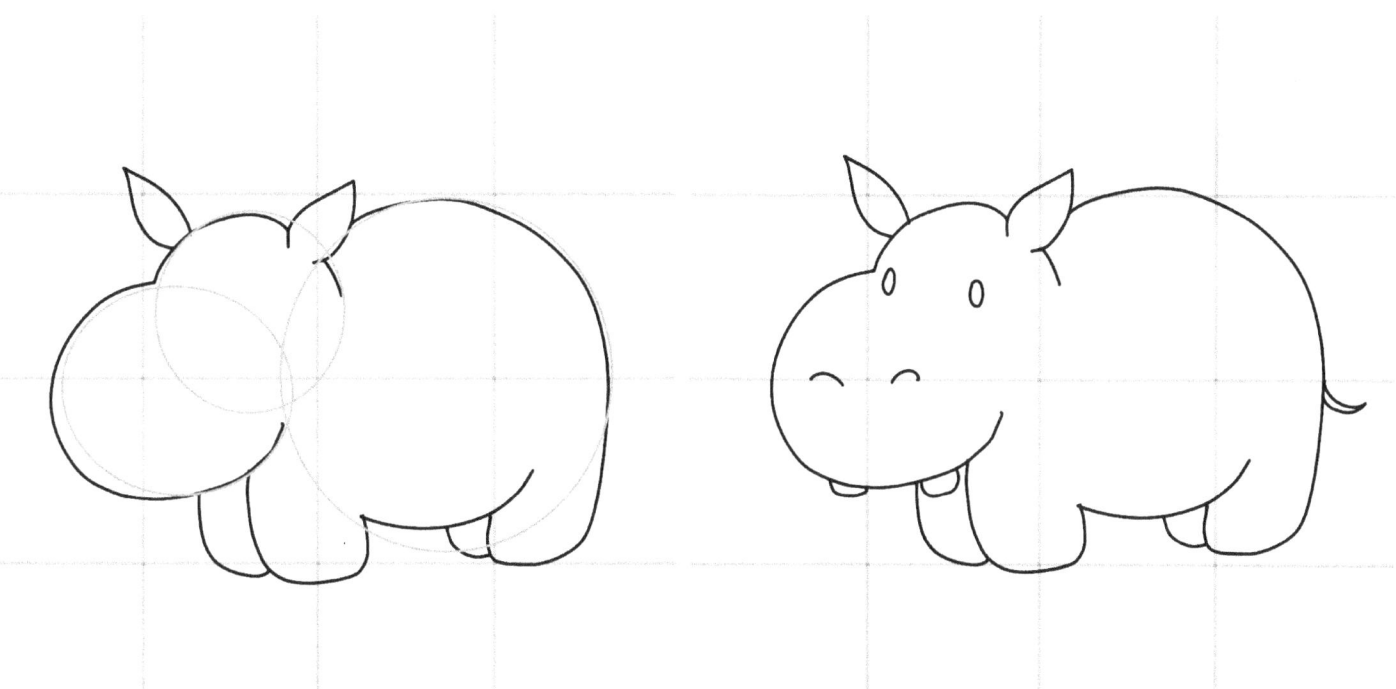

TRY it HERE!

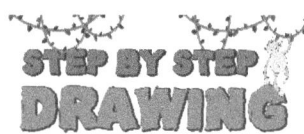

Hippo

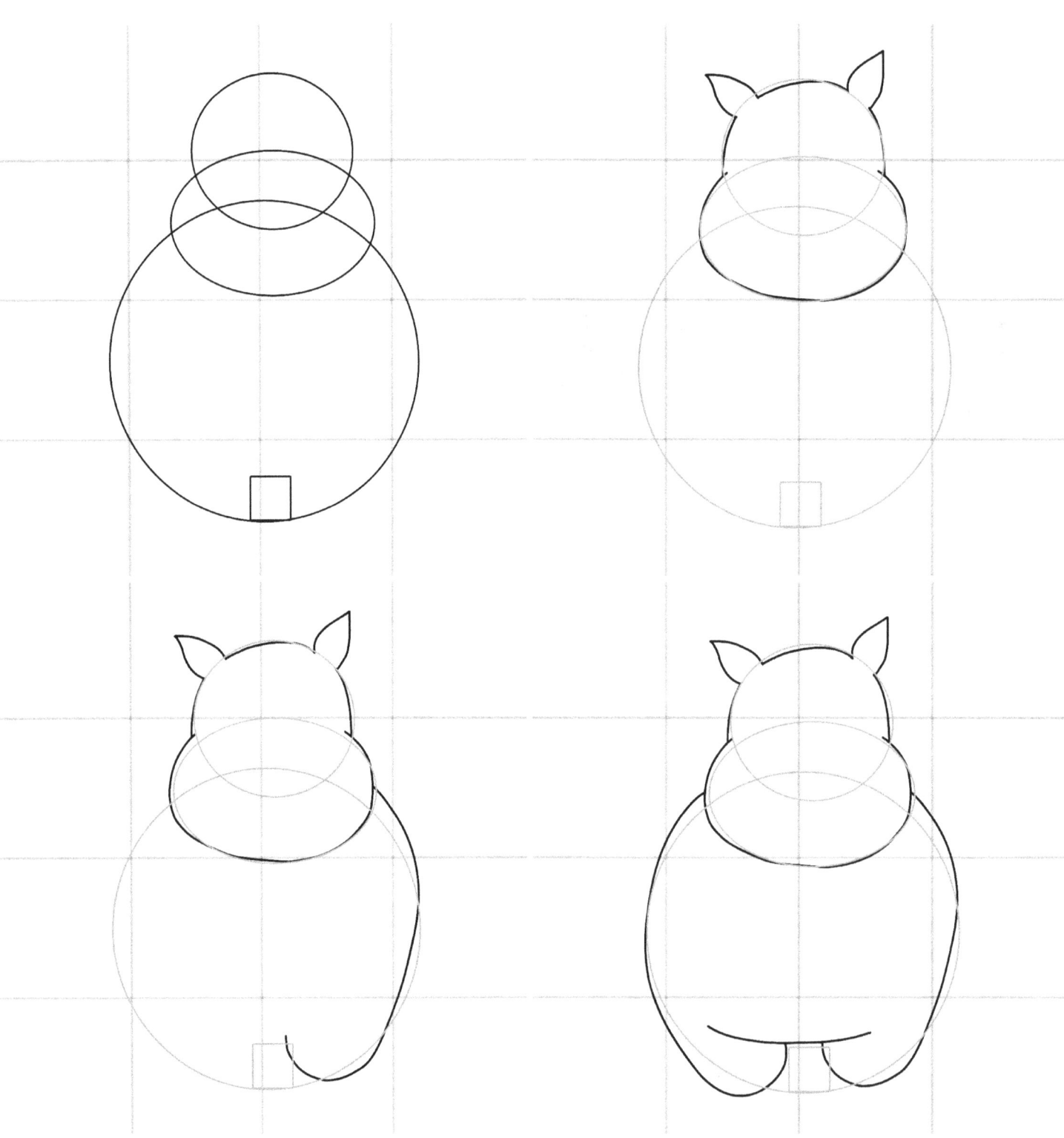

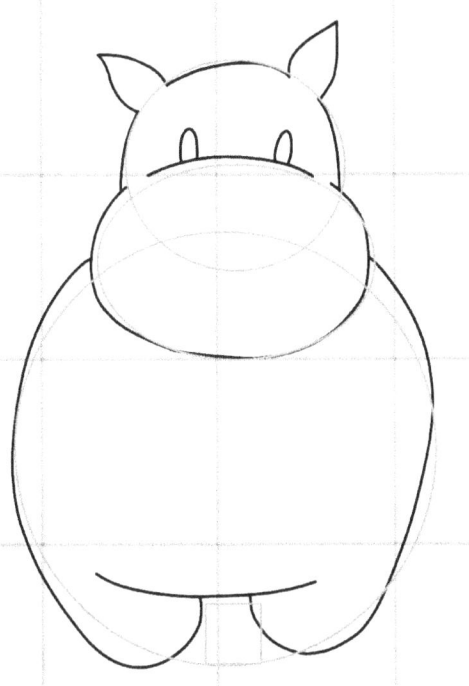
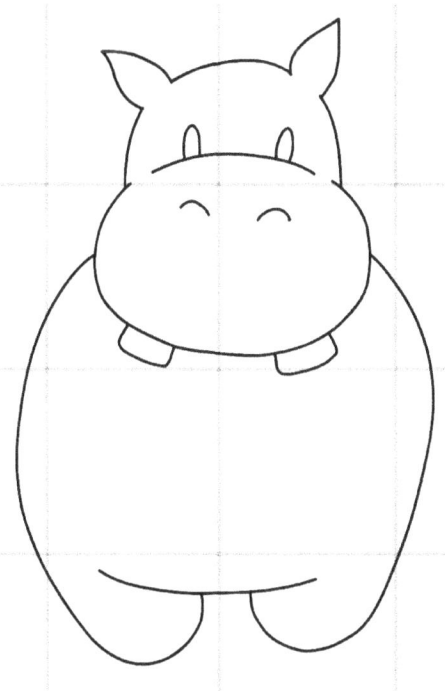

TRY it HERE!

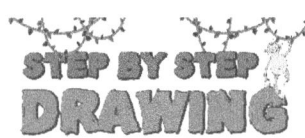

IGUANA

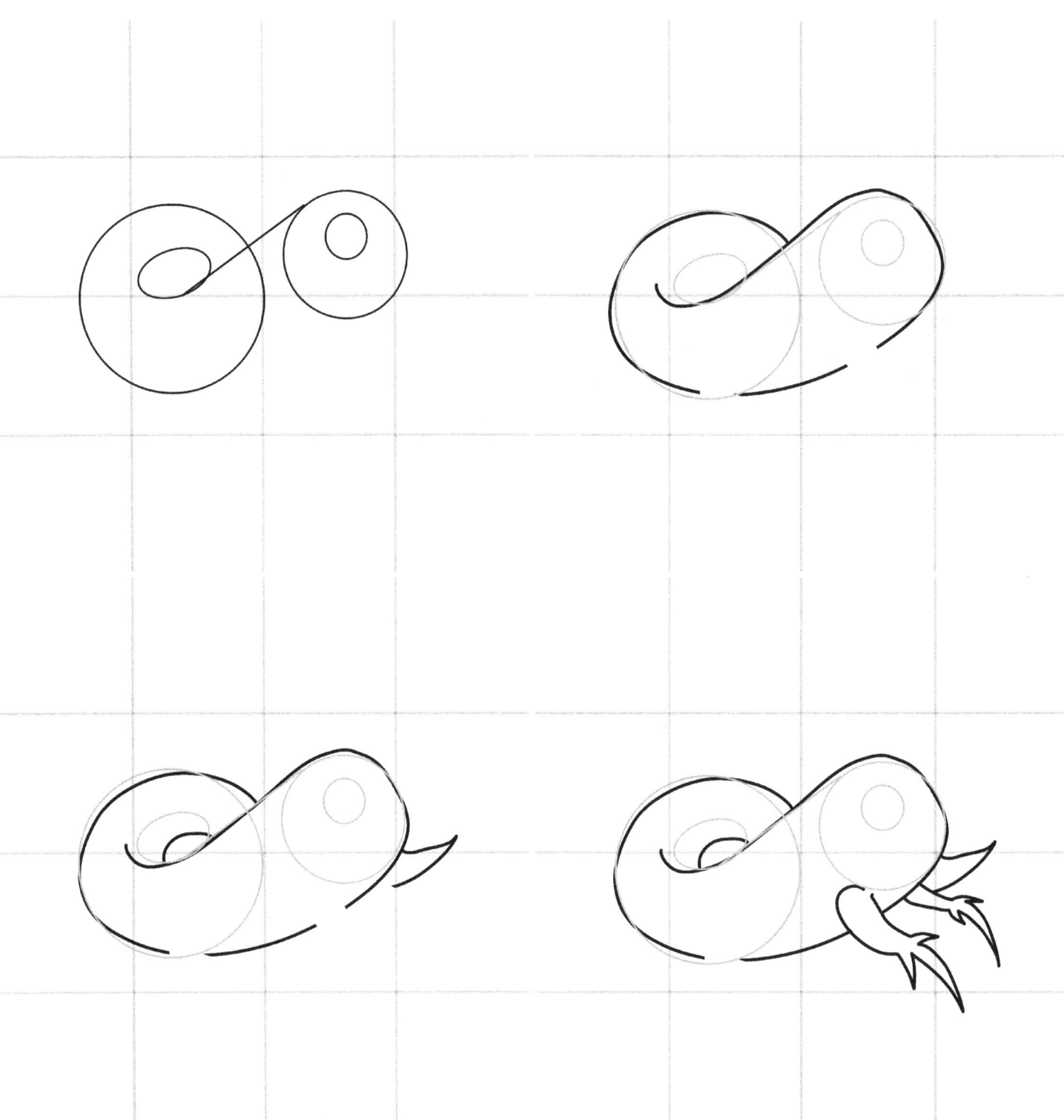

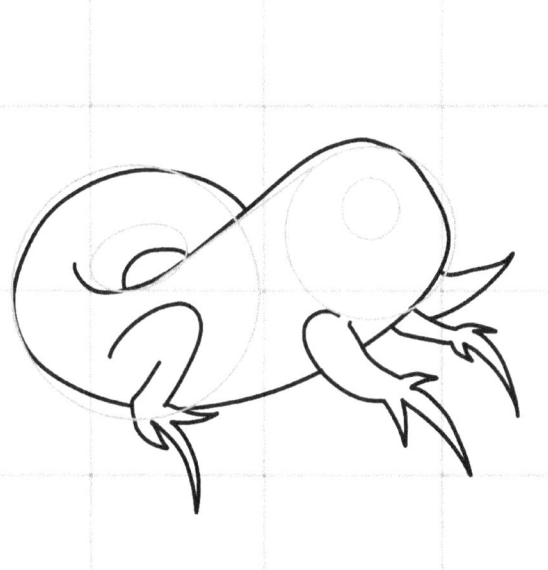
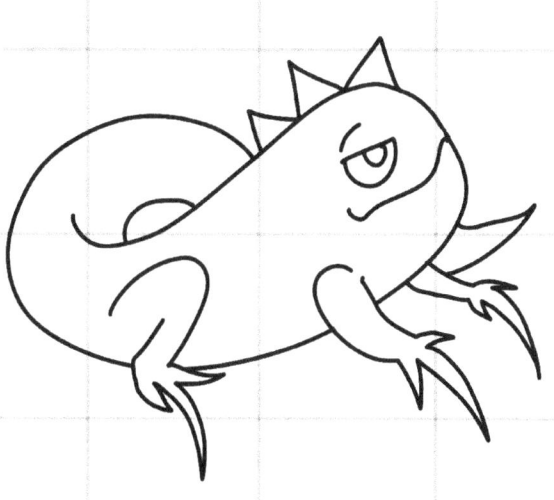

TRY it HERE!

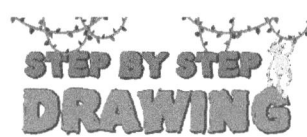

KANGAROO

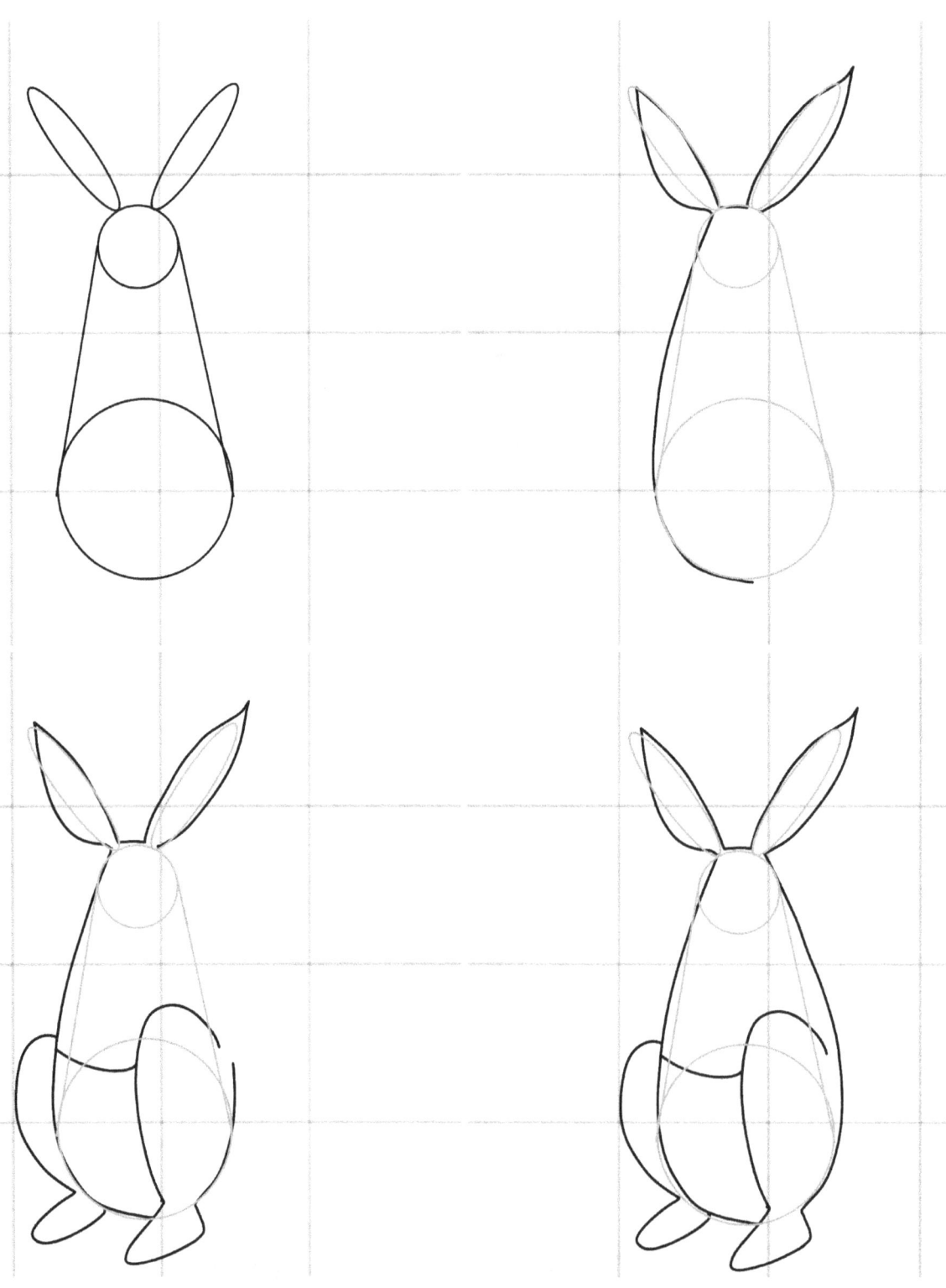

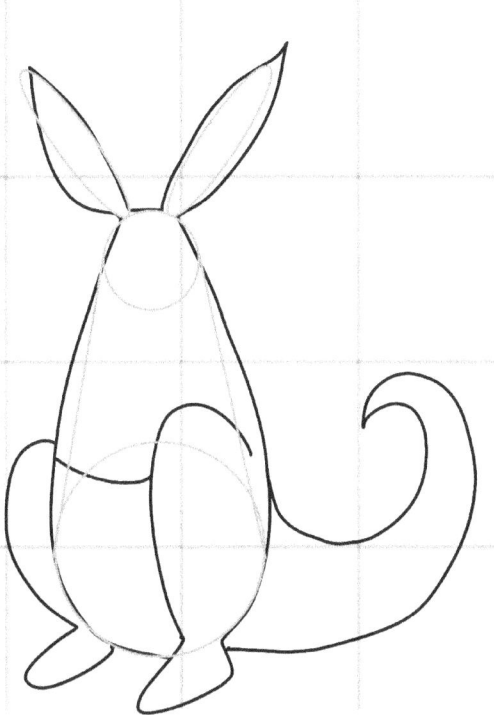 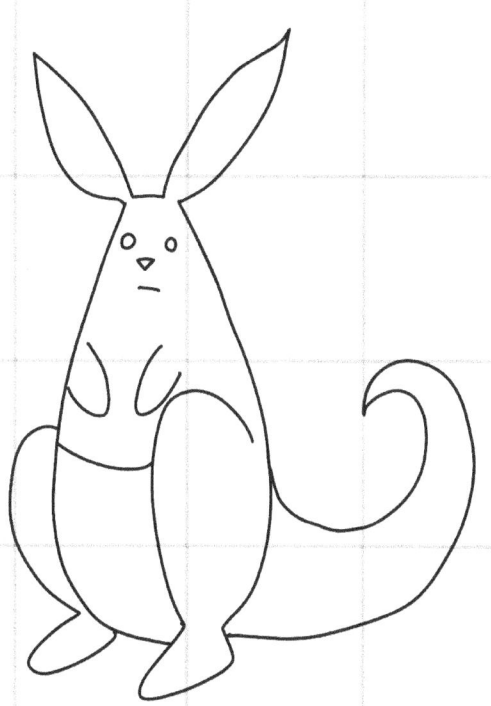

TRY iT HERE!

 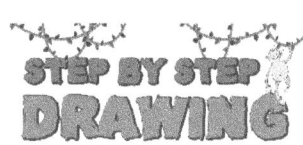

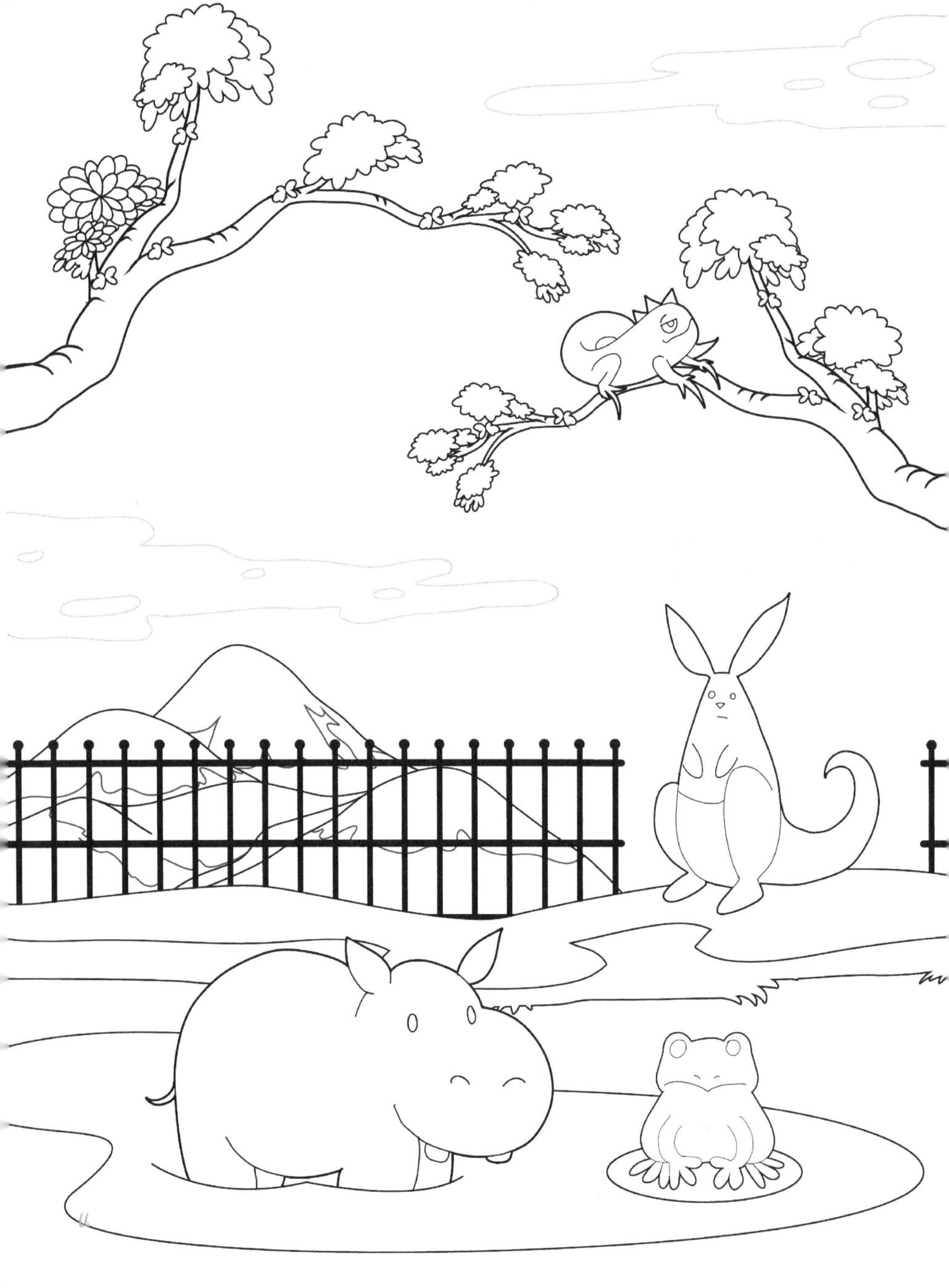

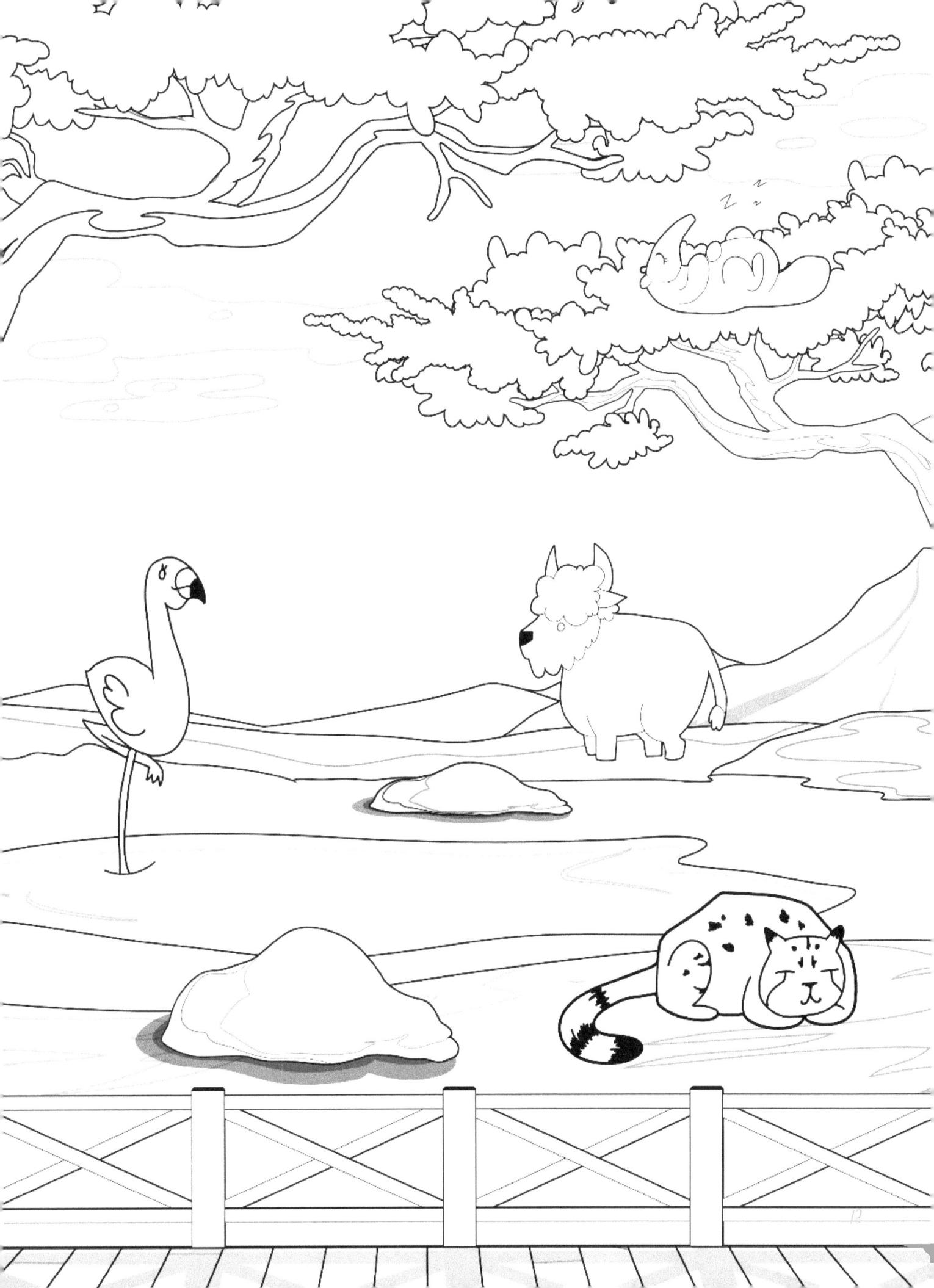

kinkajou

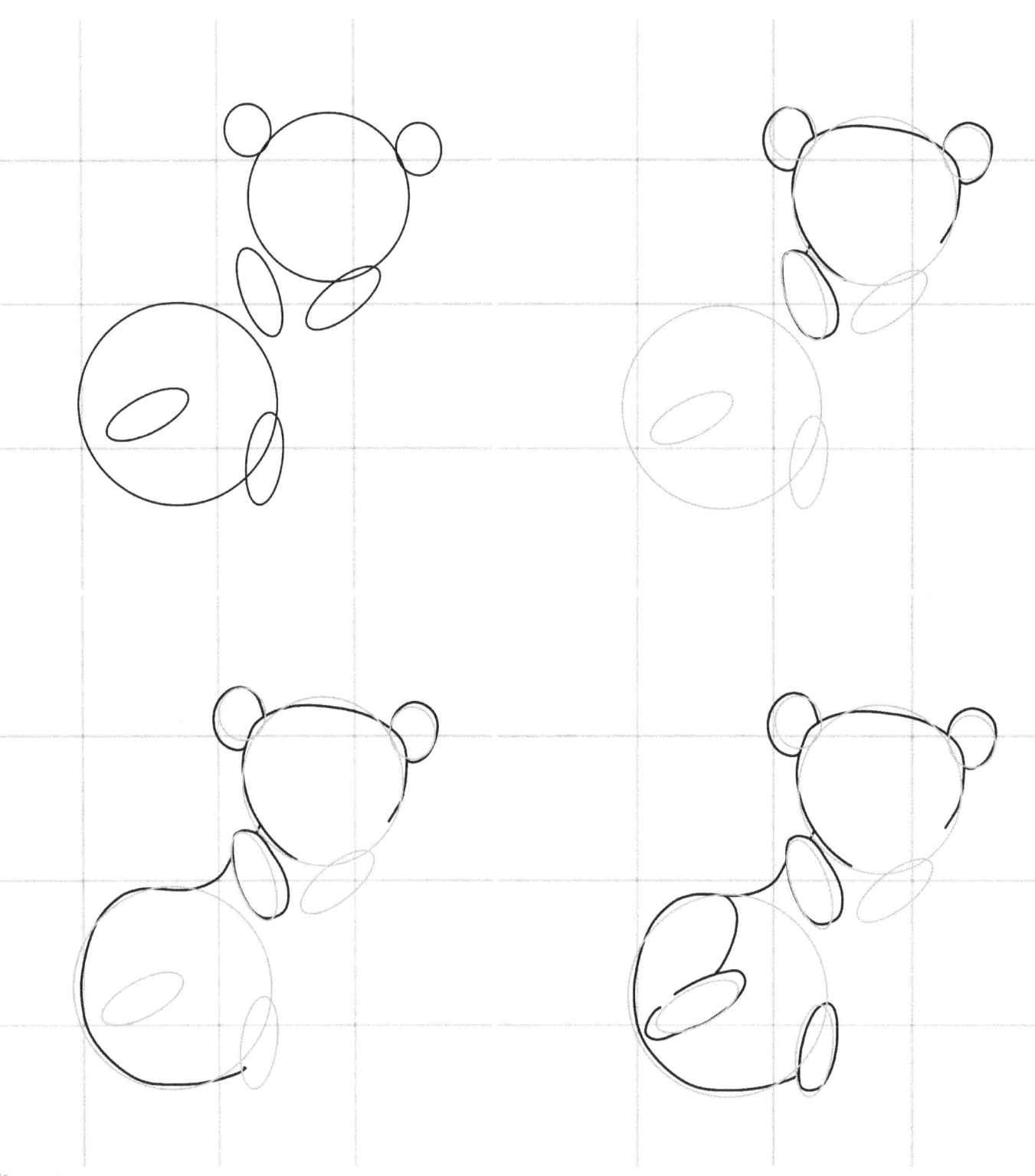

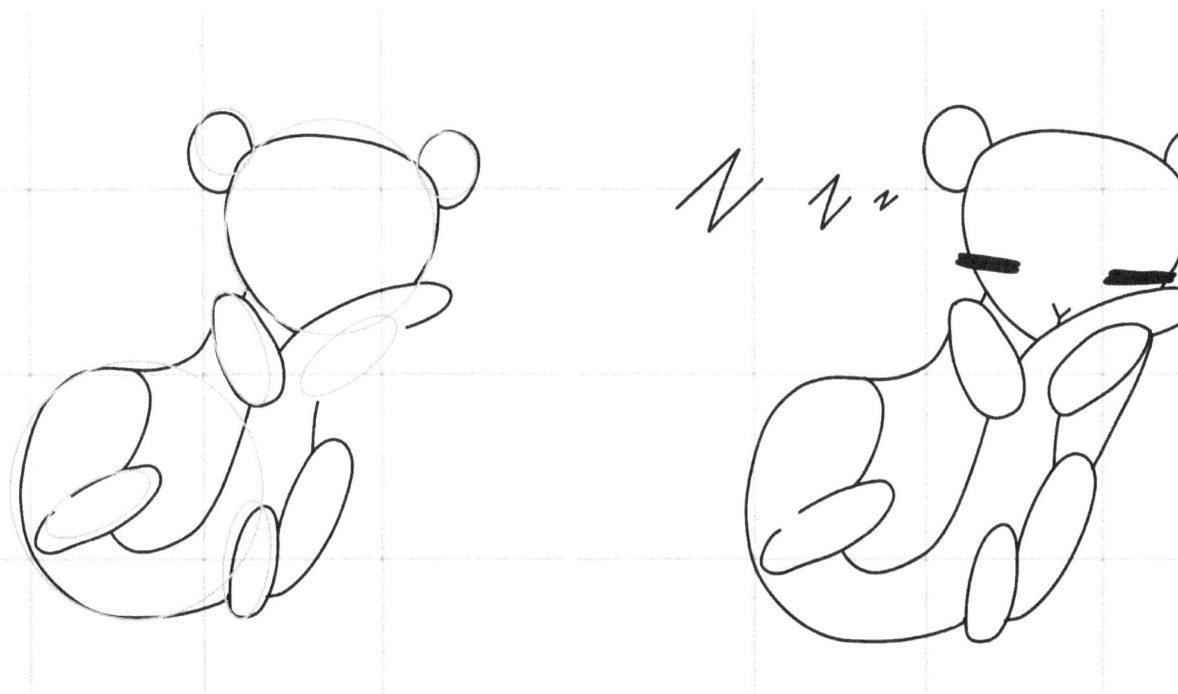

TRY it HERE!

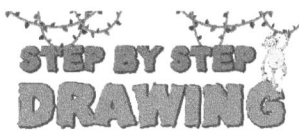

KINKAJOU

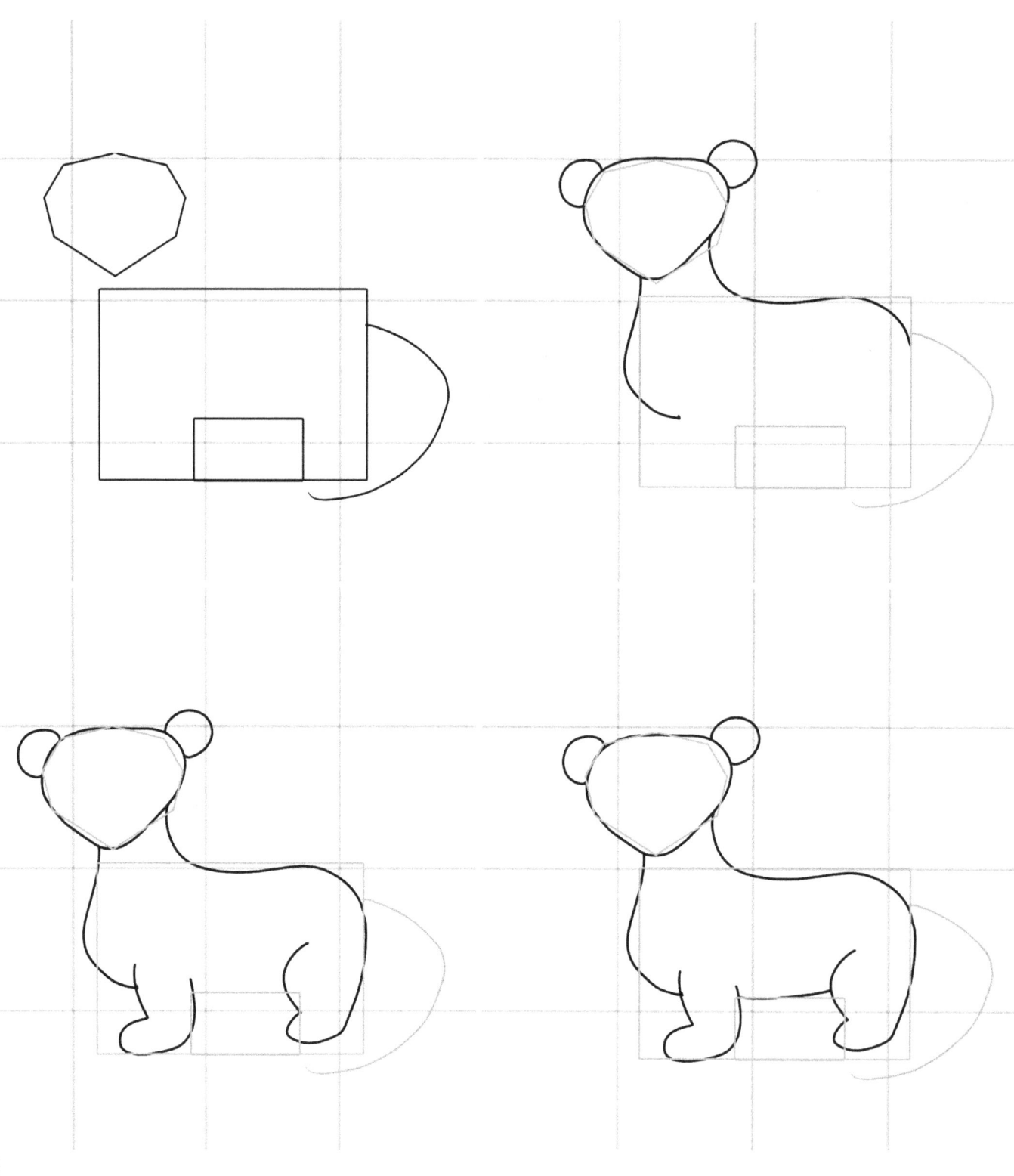

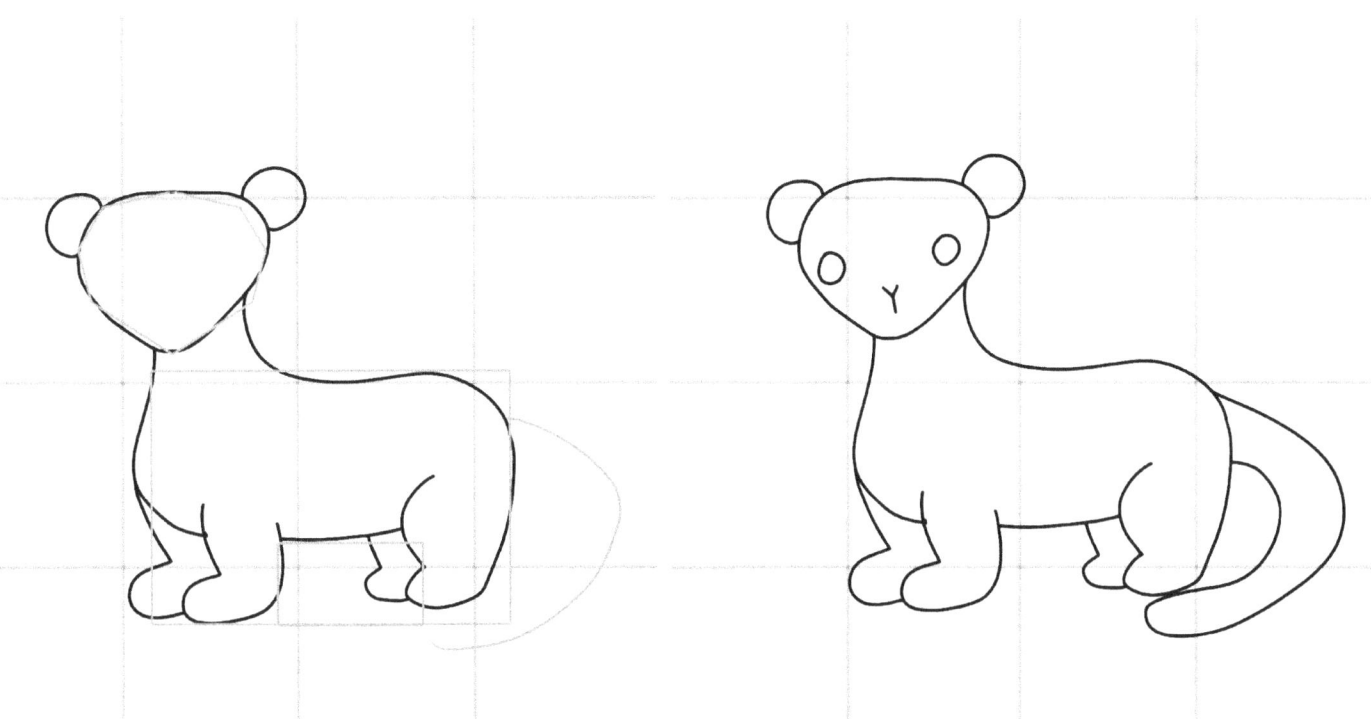

TRY it HERE!

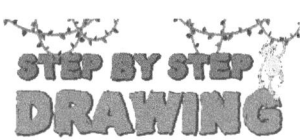

kiwi

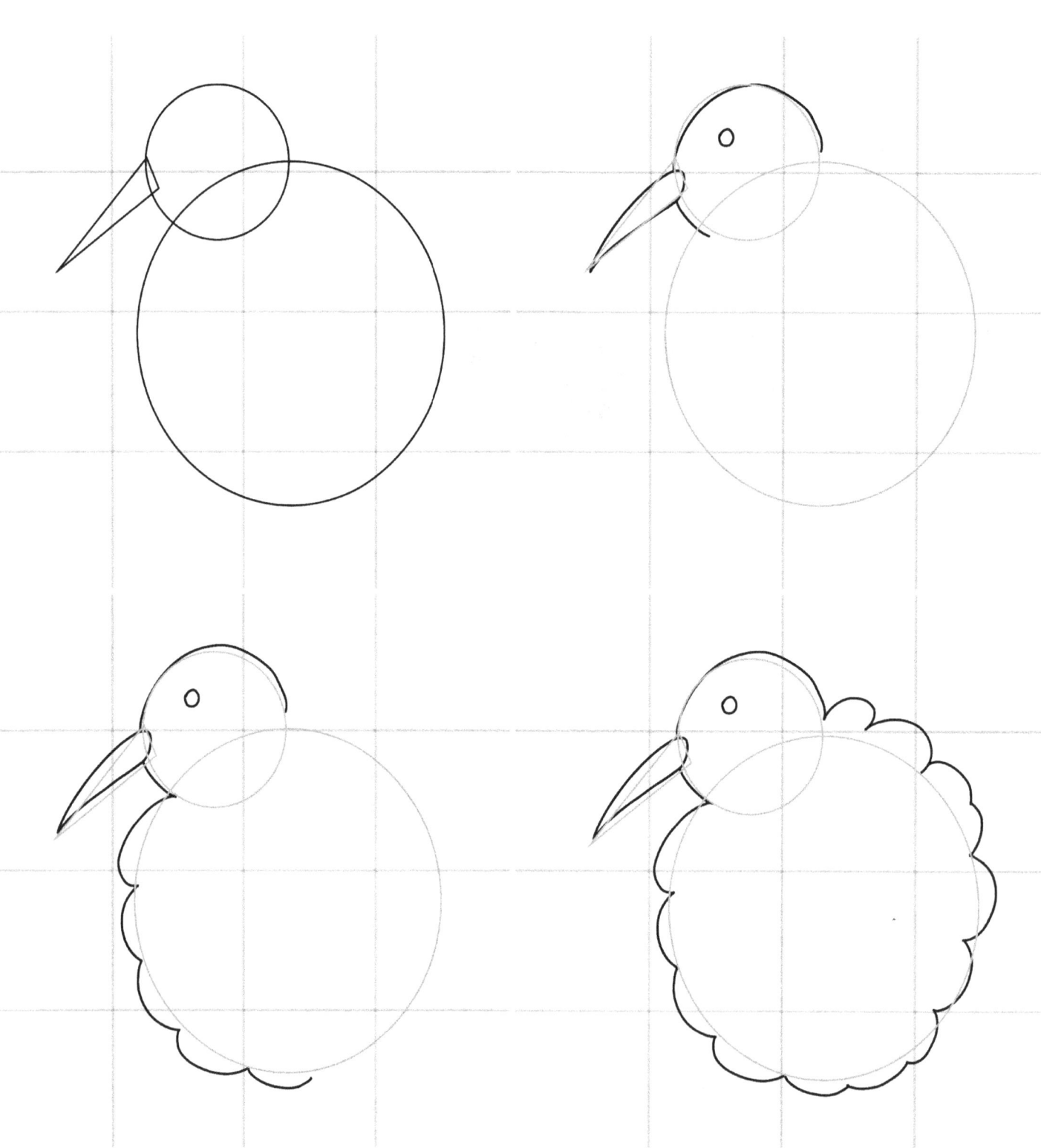

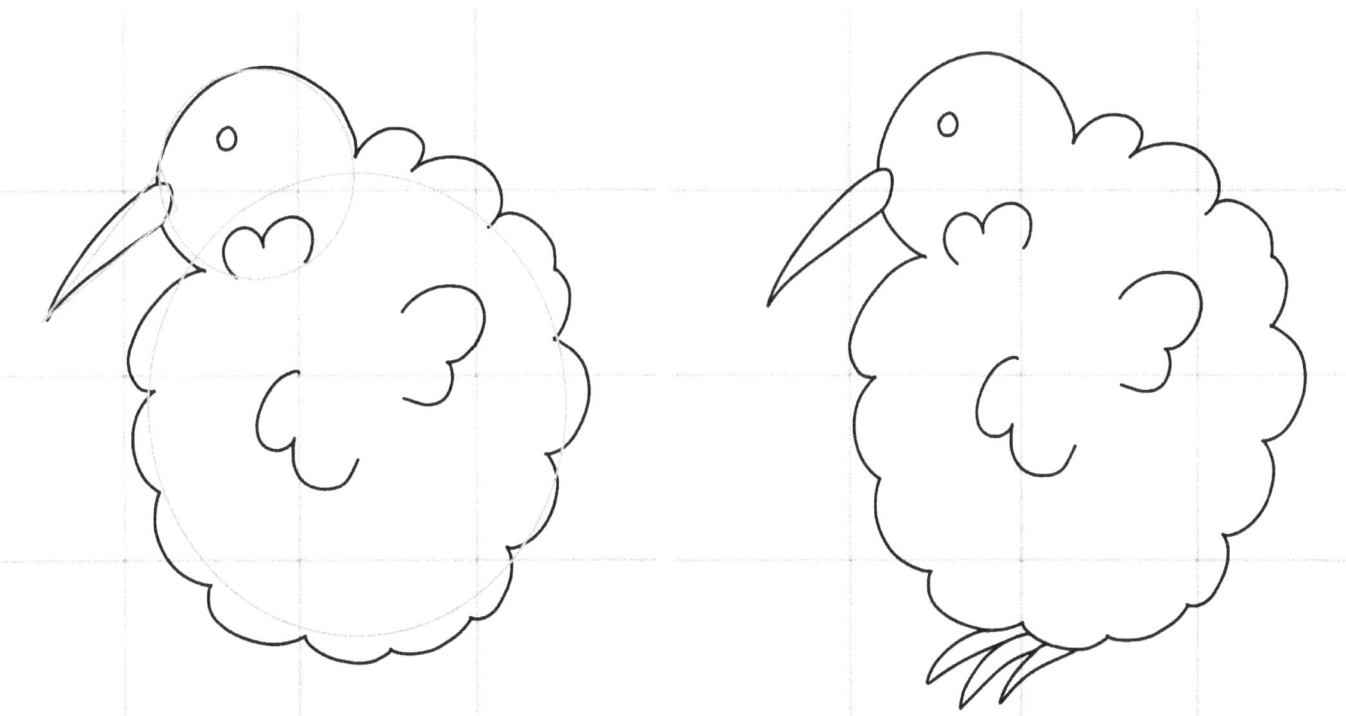

TRY iT HERE!

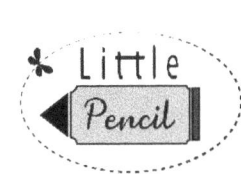
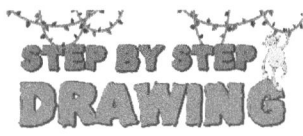

kiwi

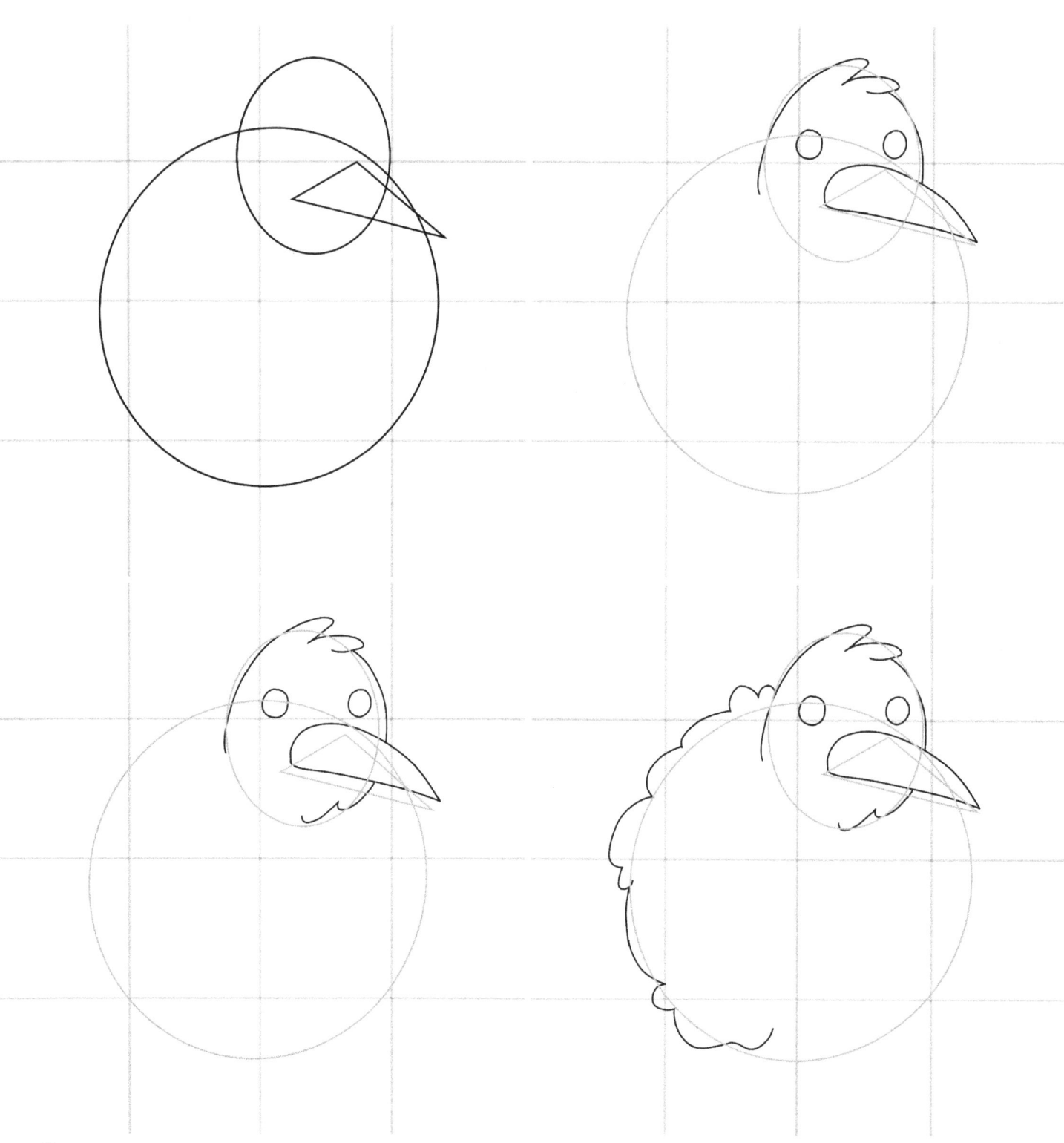

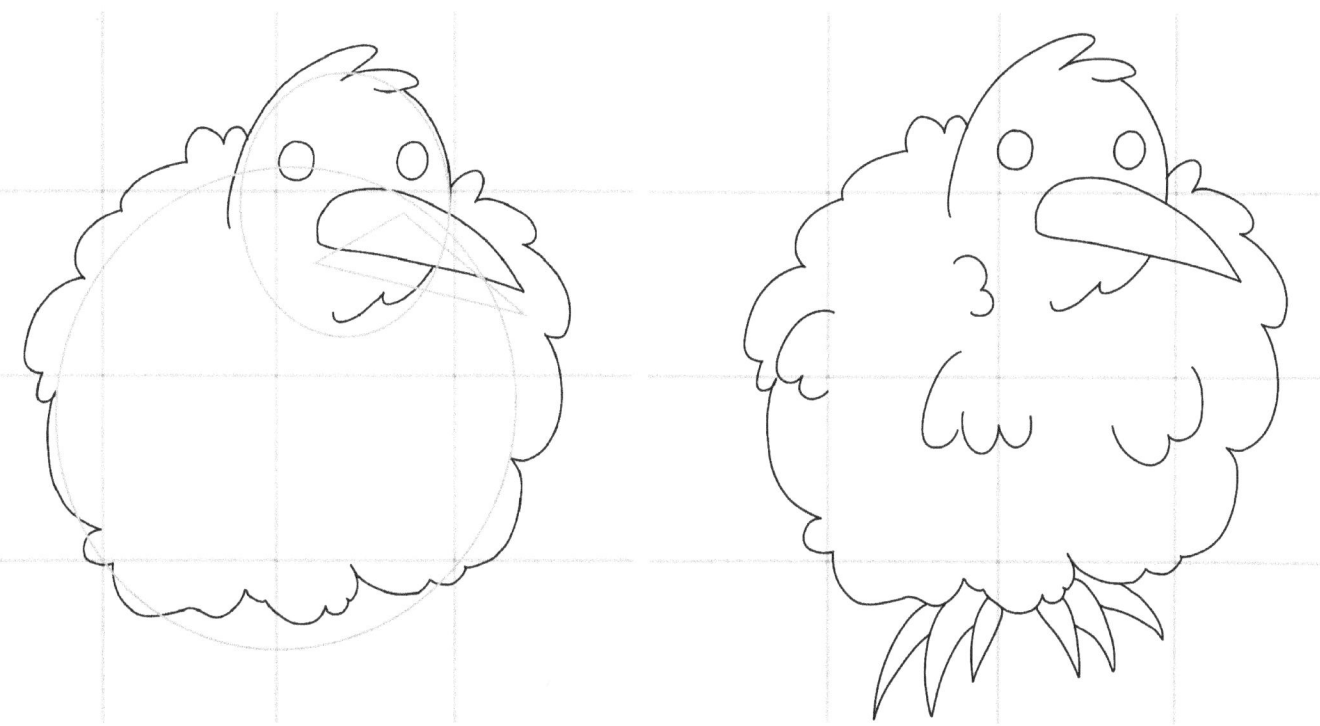

TRY IT HERE!

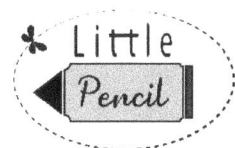

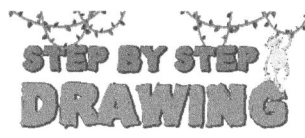

Lion

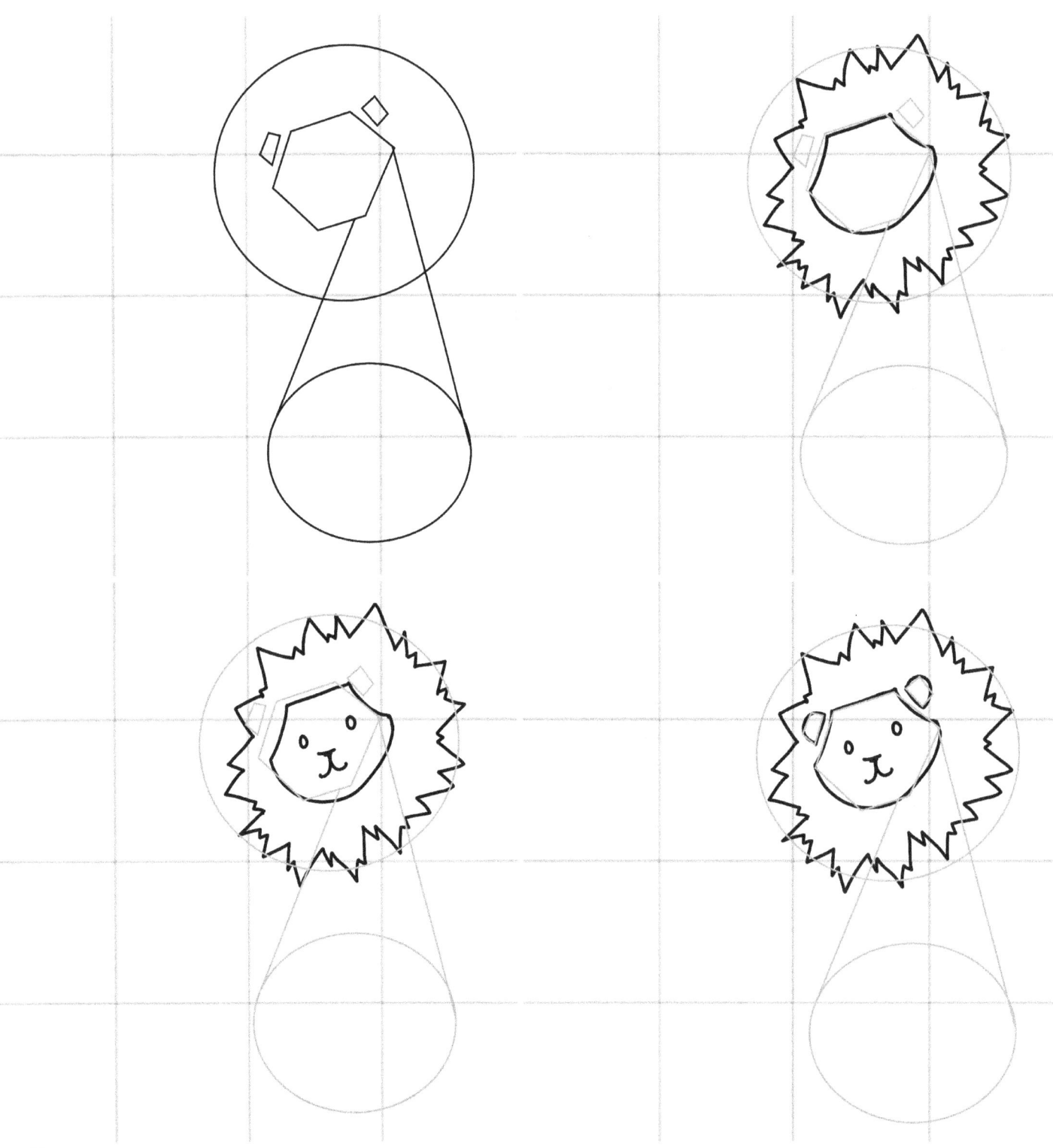

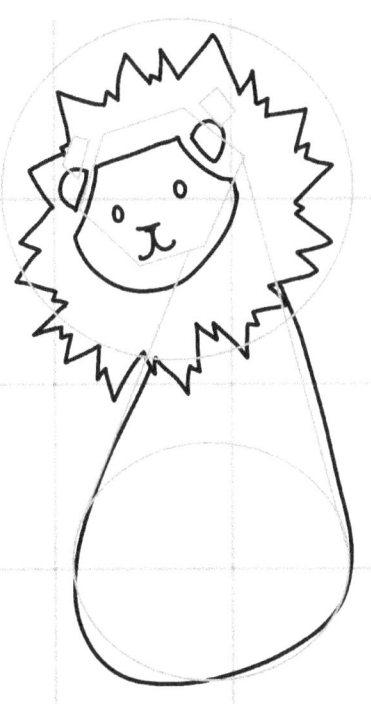

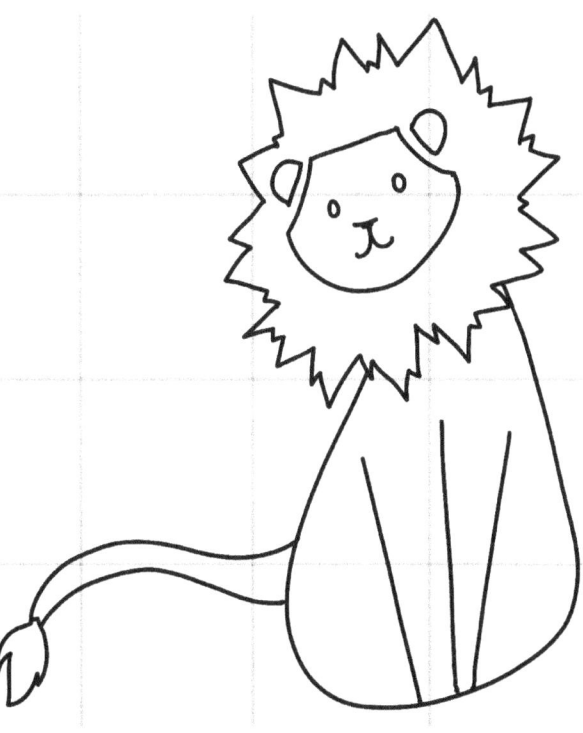

TRY iT HERE!

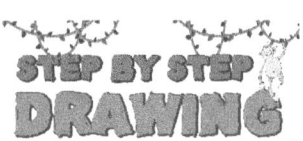

Lion

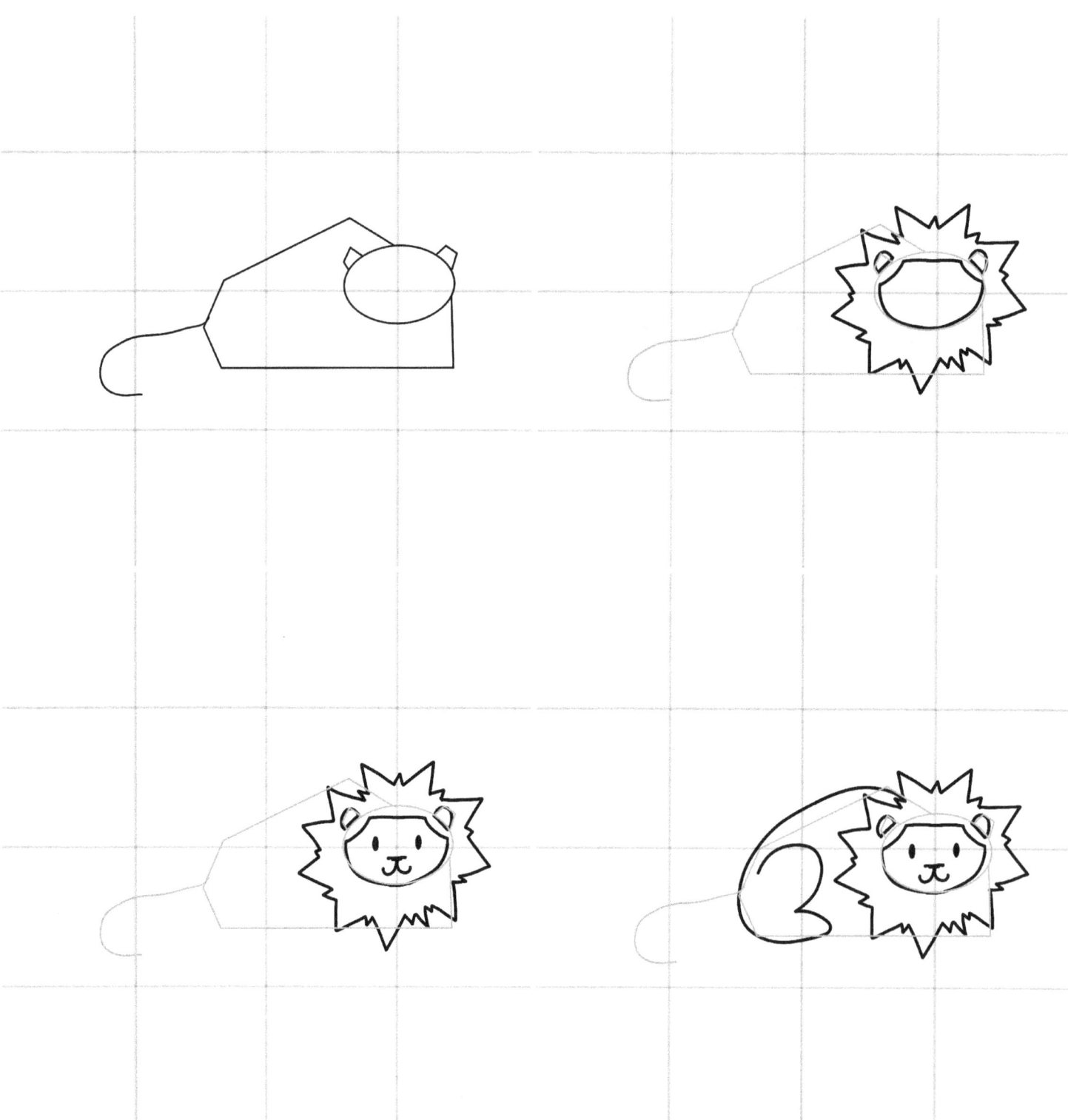

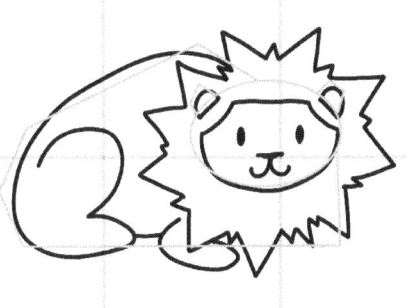

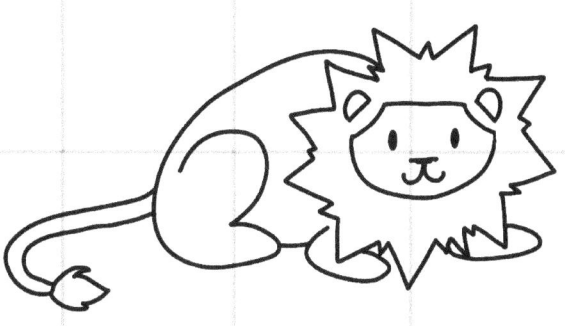

TRY iT HERE!

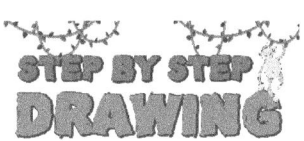

MONKEY

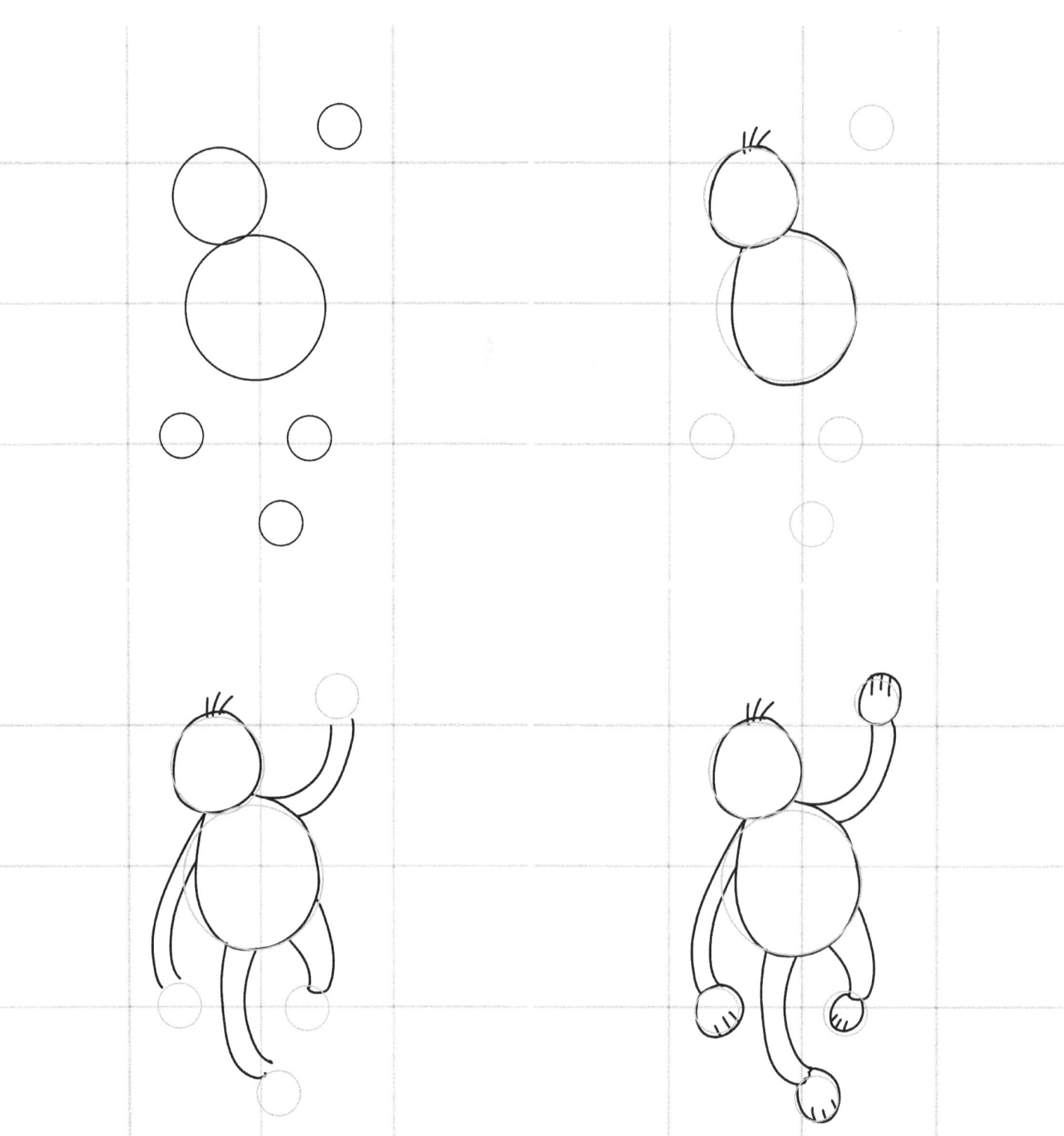

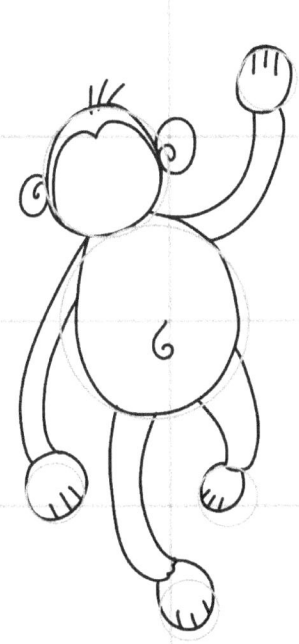
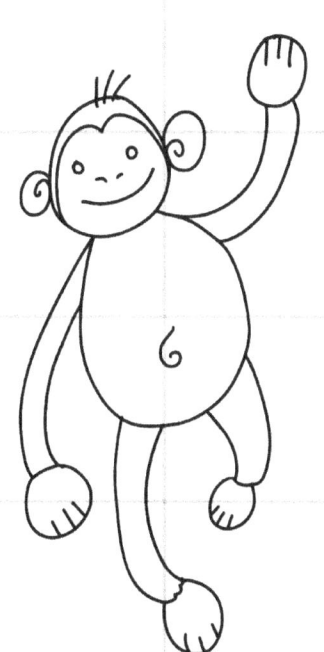

TRY iT HERE!

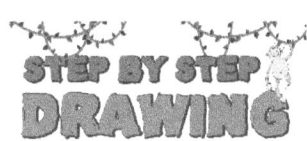

ORYX

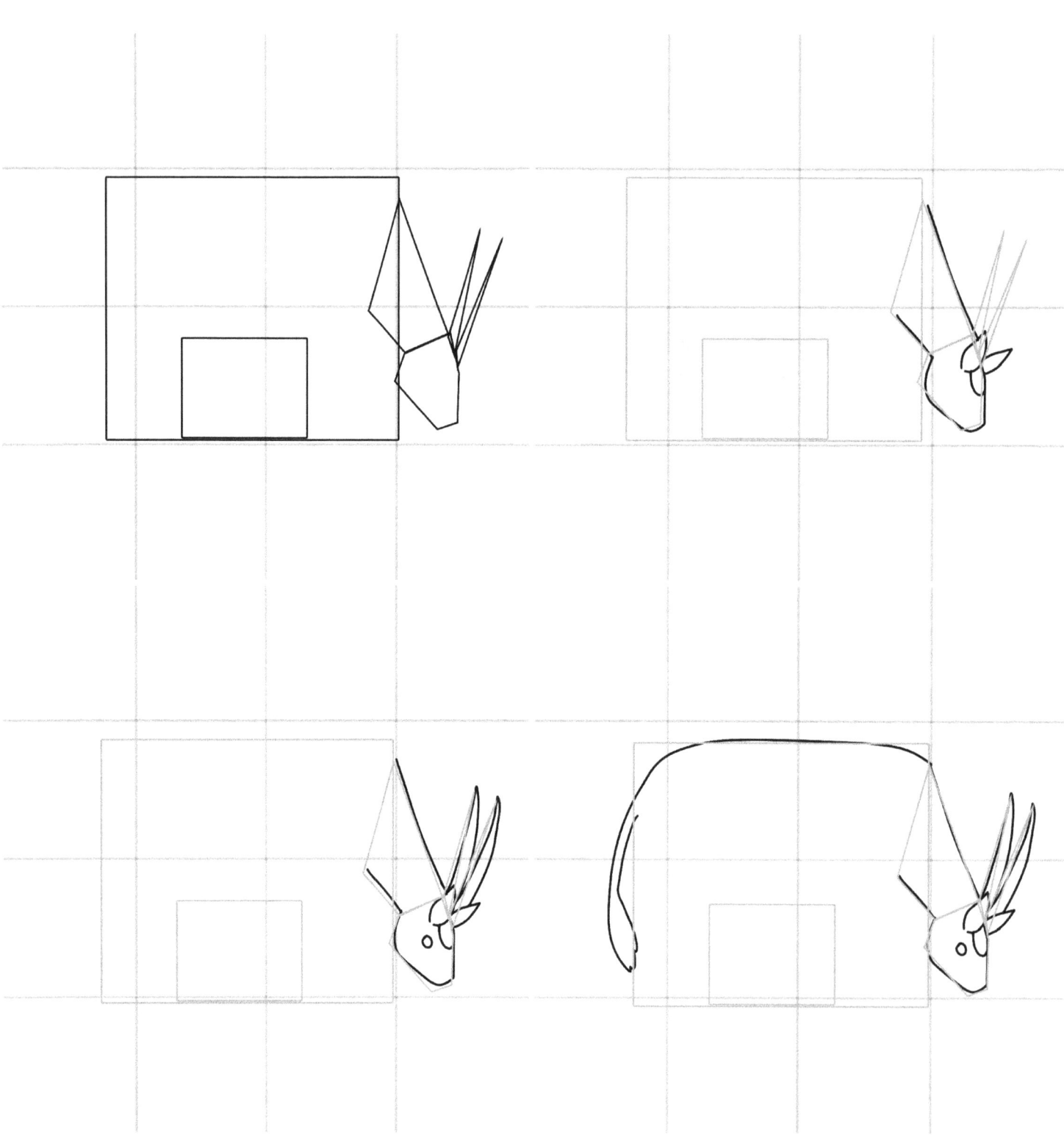

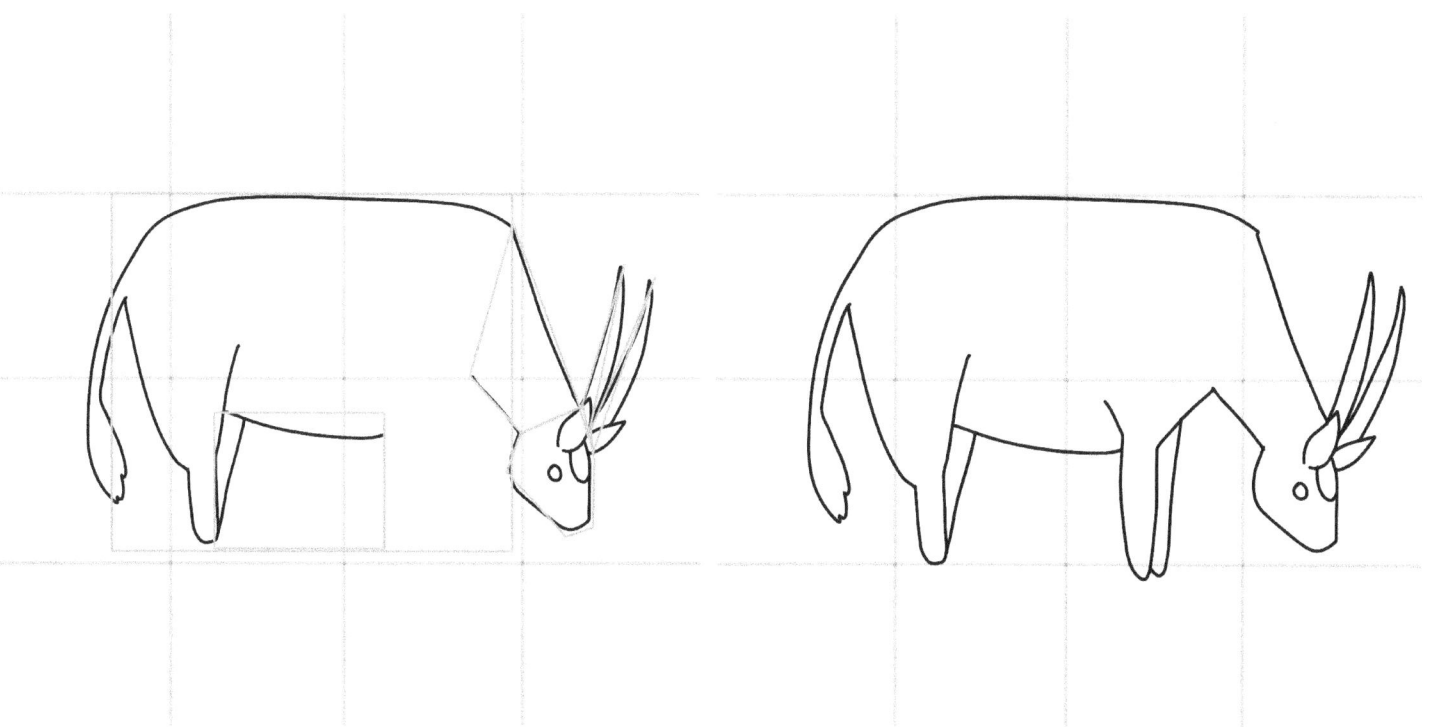

TRY it HERE!

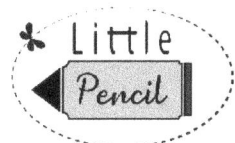

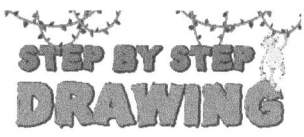

ORYX

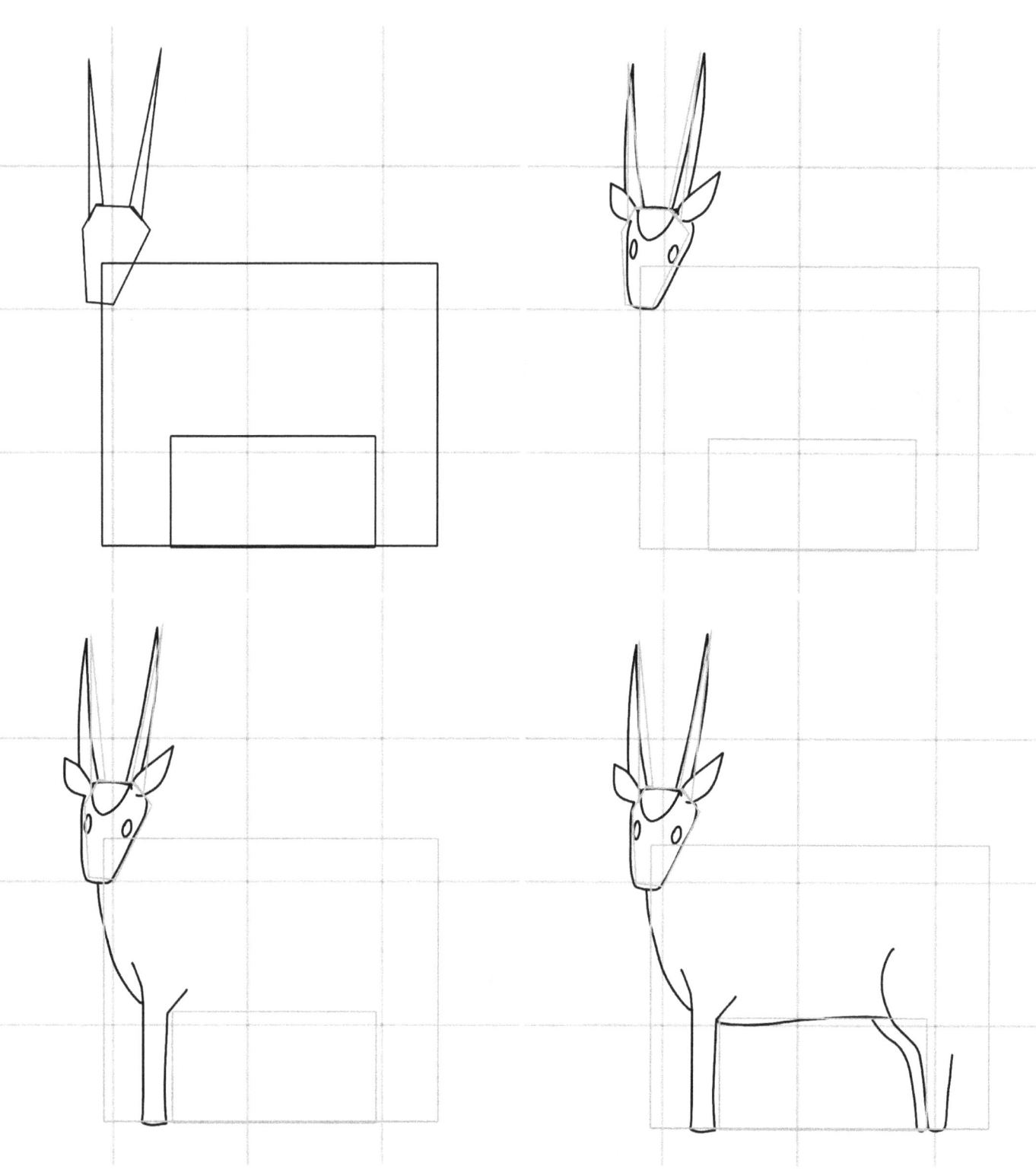

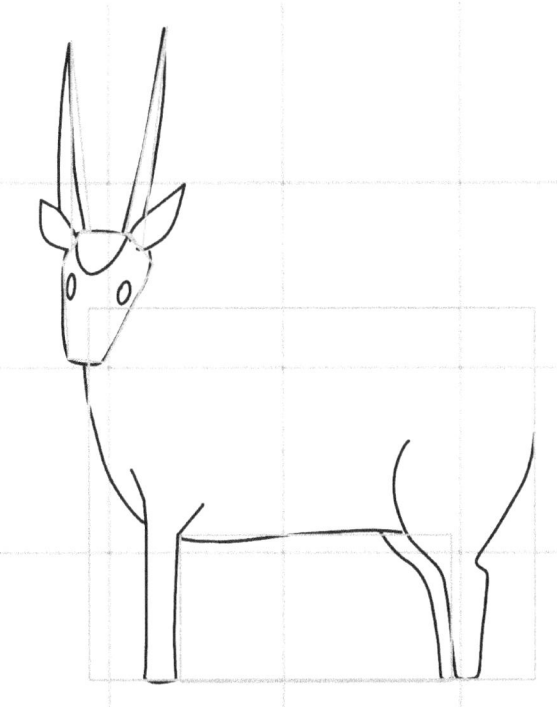

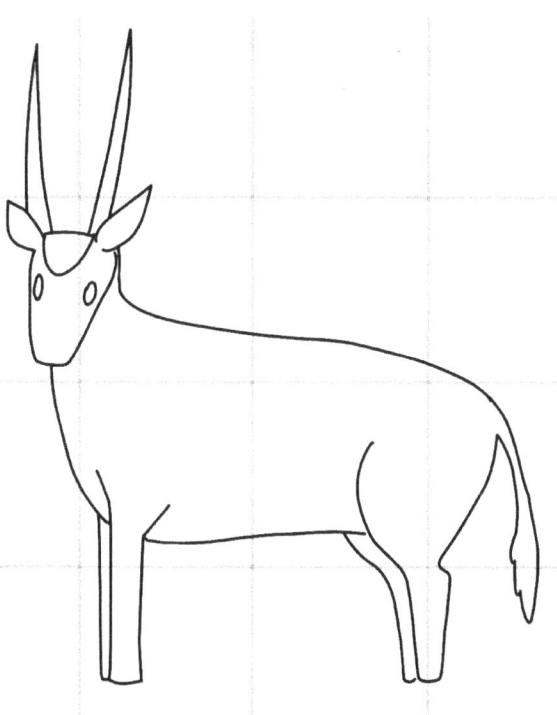

TRY iT HERE!

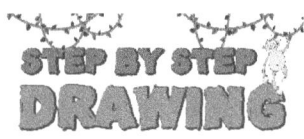

PANDA

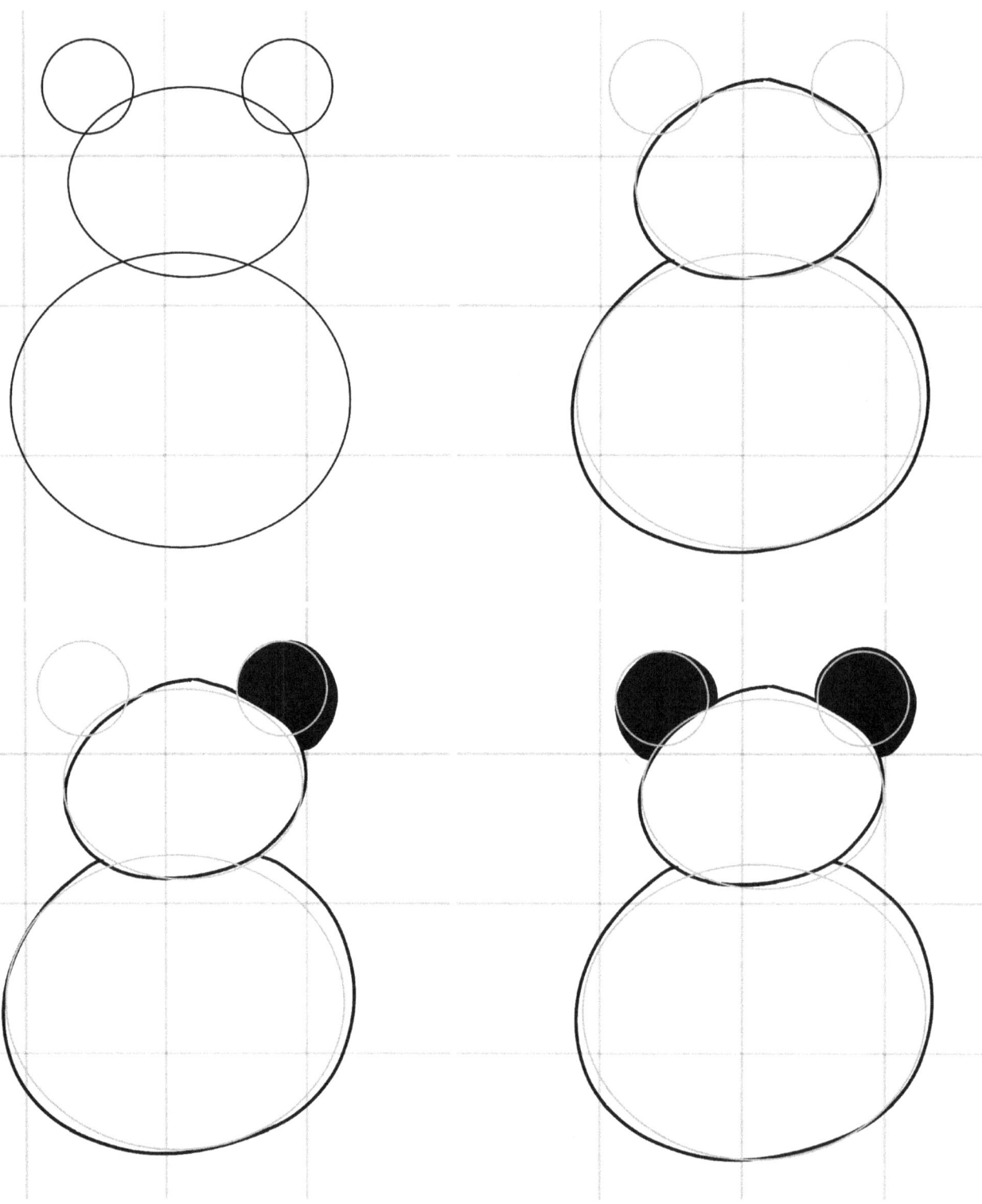

86

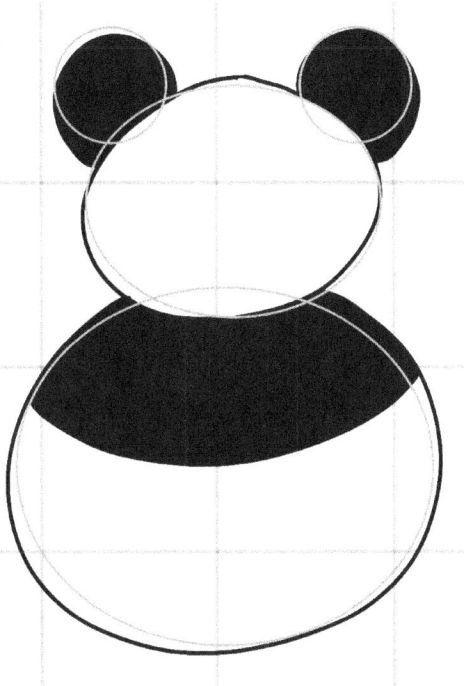
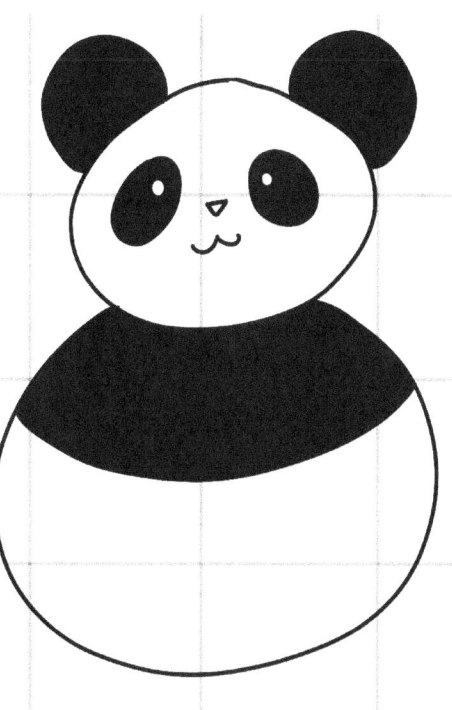

TRY it HERE!

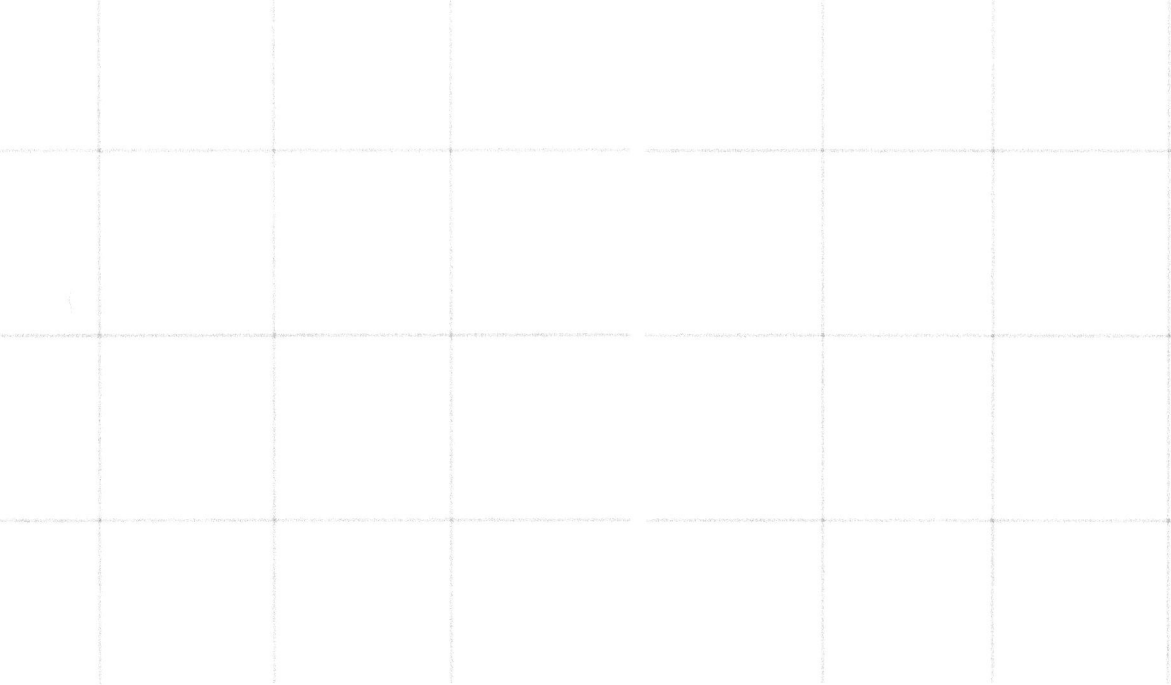

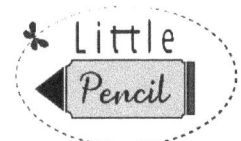
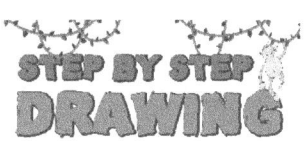

PANDA

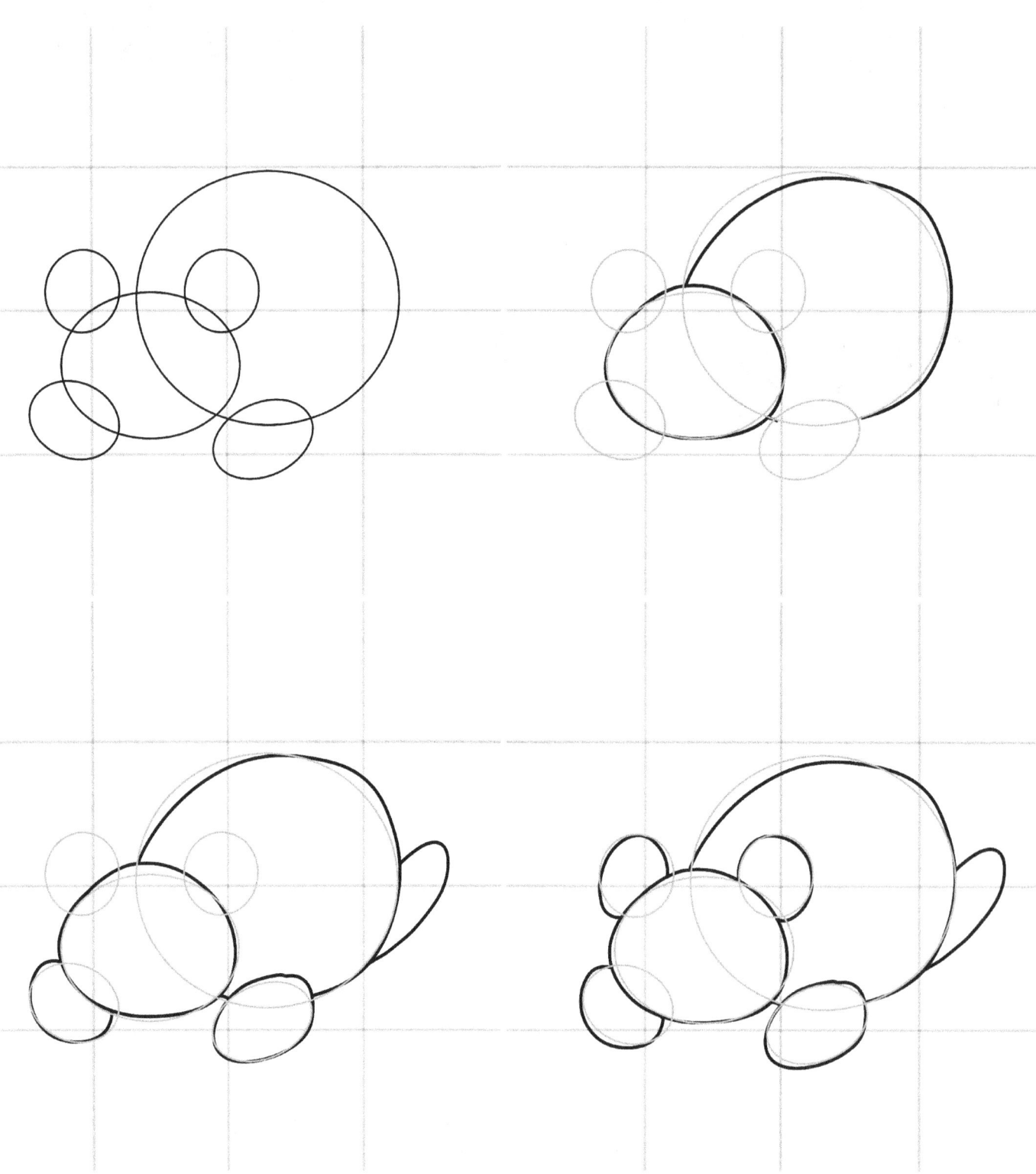

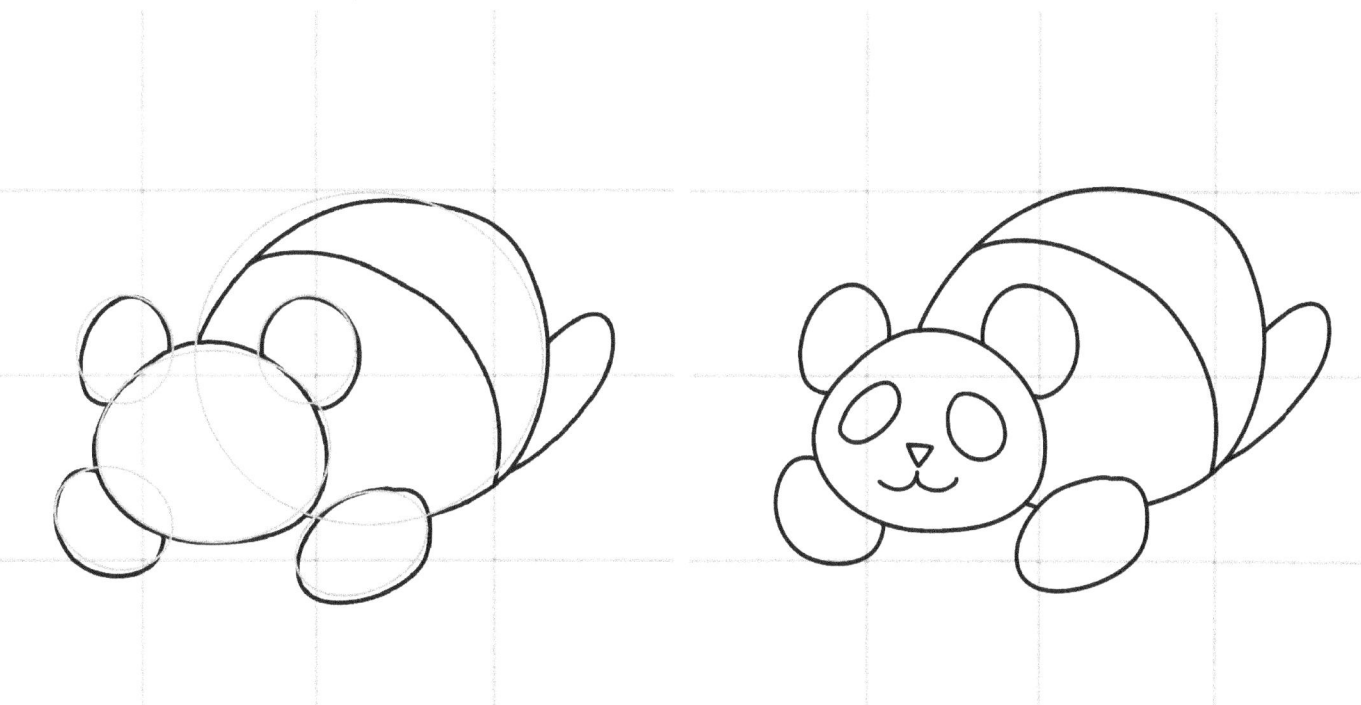

TRY IT HERE!

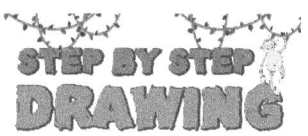

PARROT

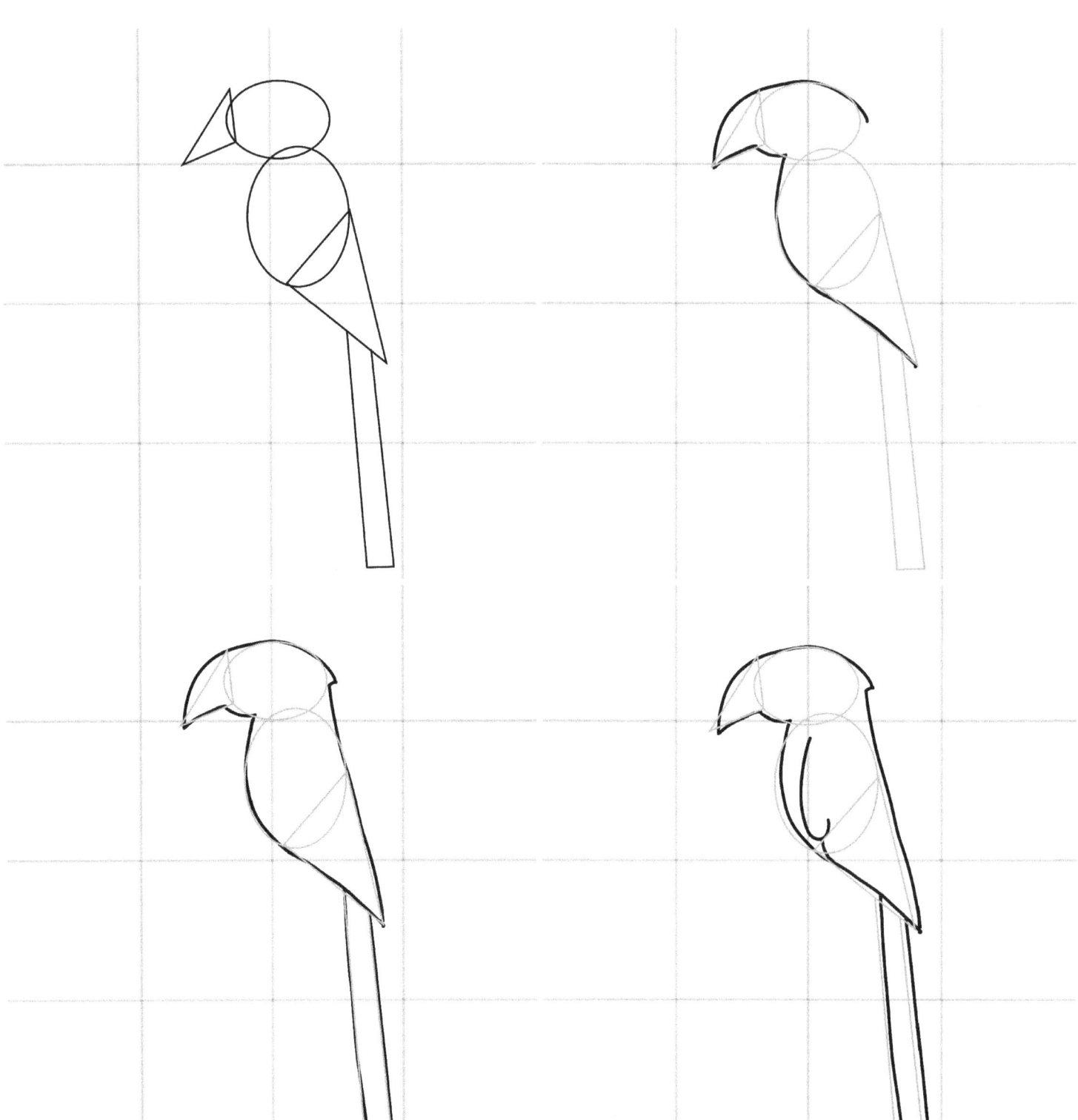

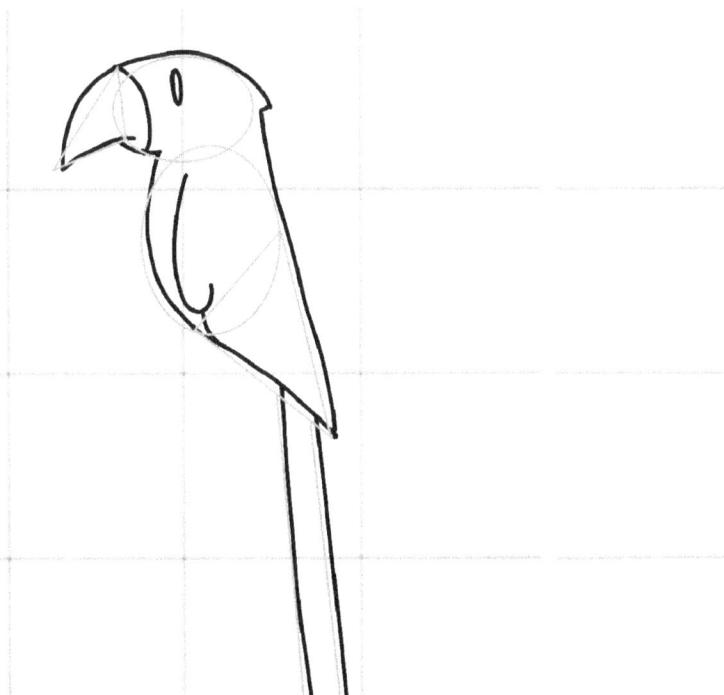
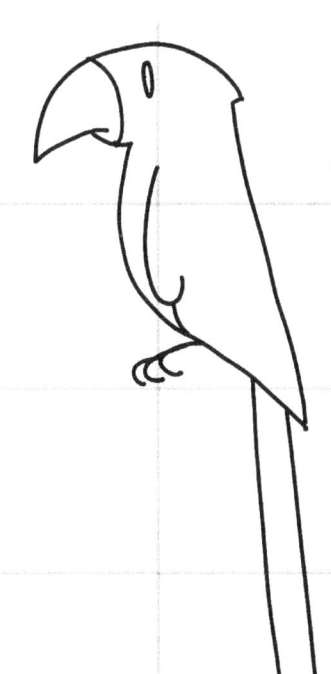

TRY it HERE!

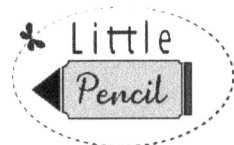
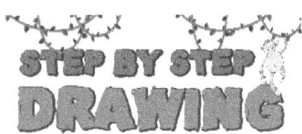

PARROT

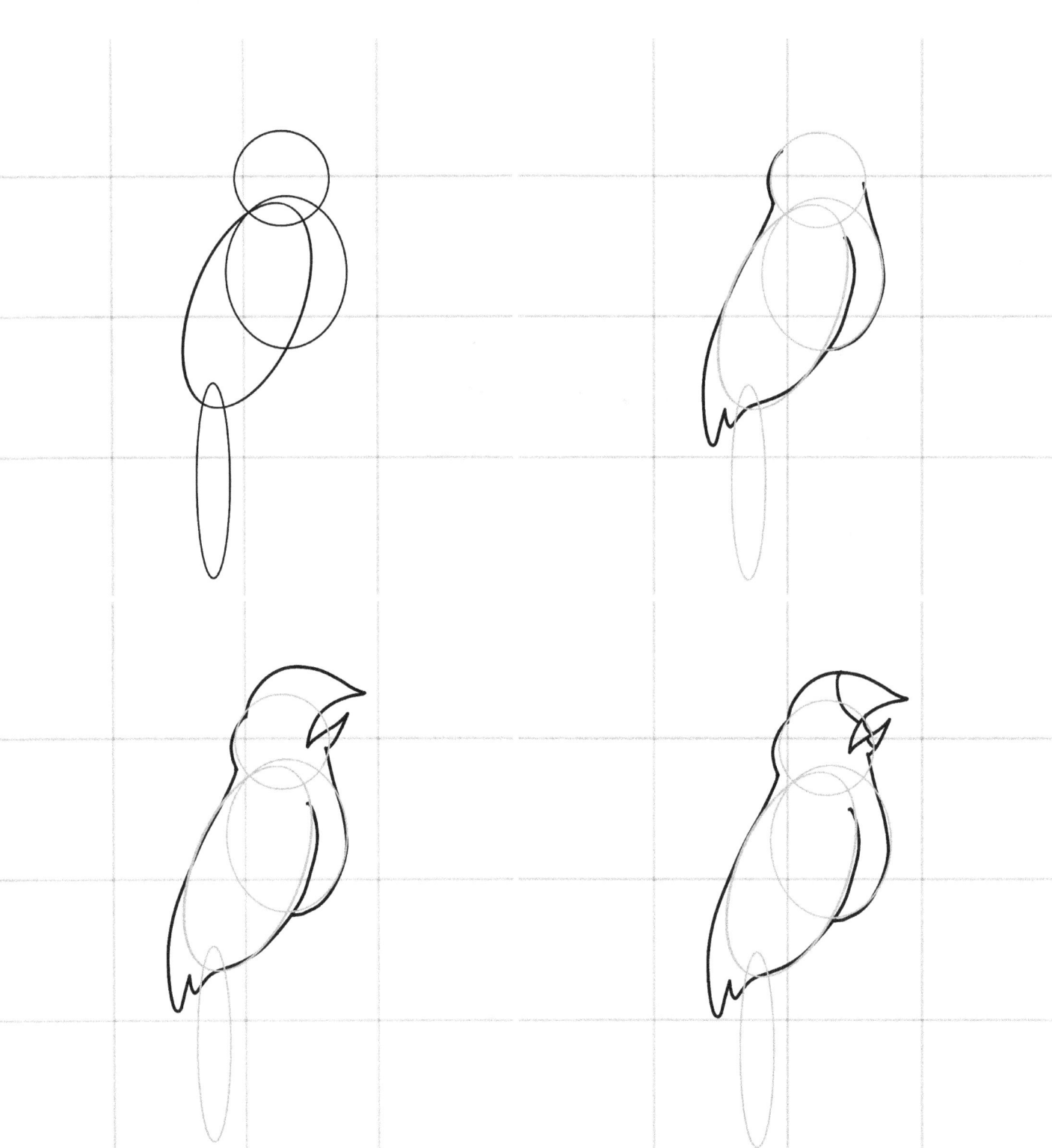

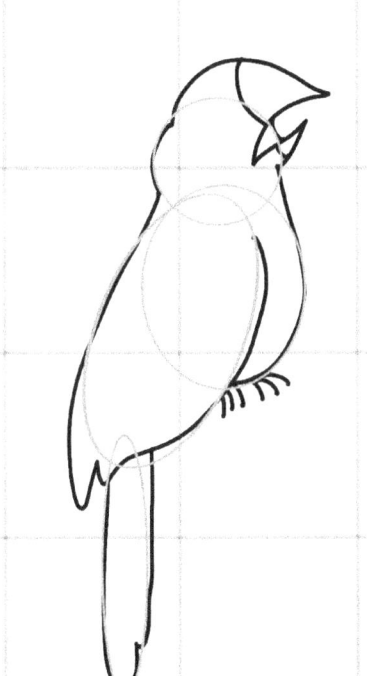

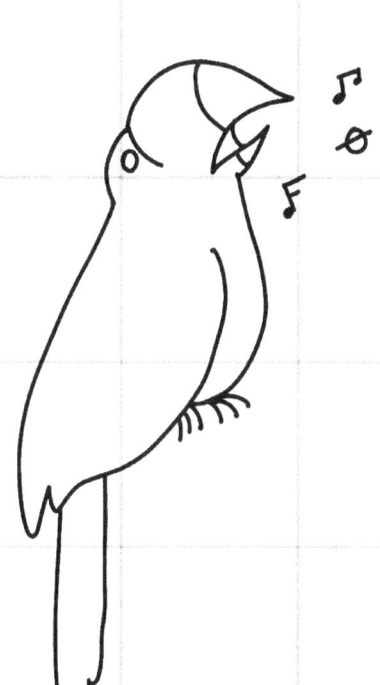

TRY it HERE!

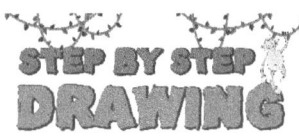

PENGUIN

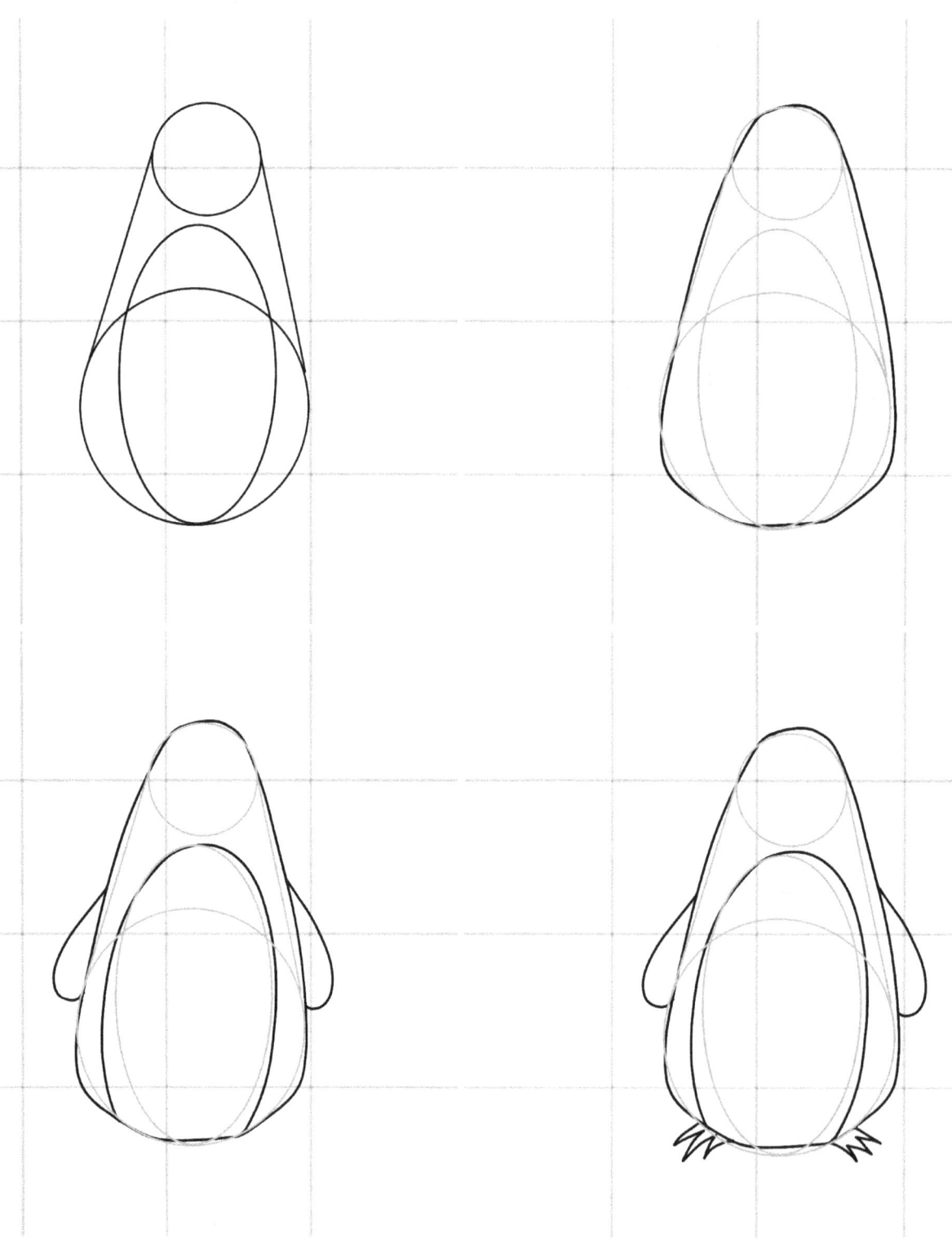

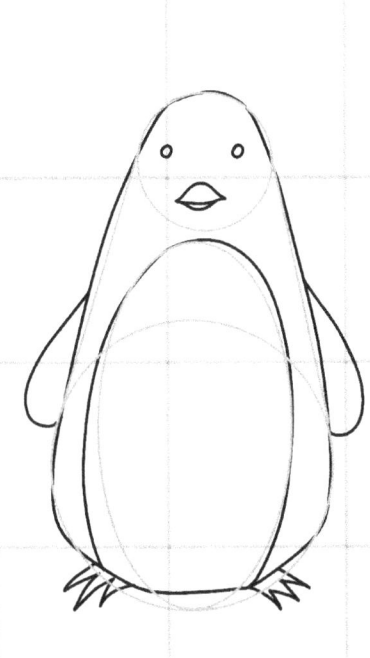

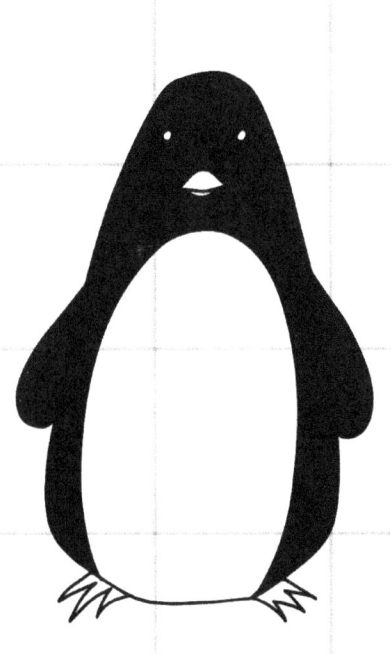

TRY it HERE!

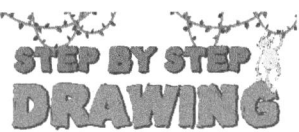

POLAR BEAR

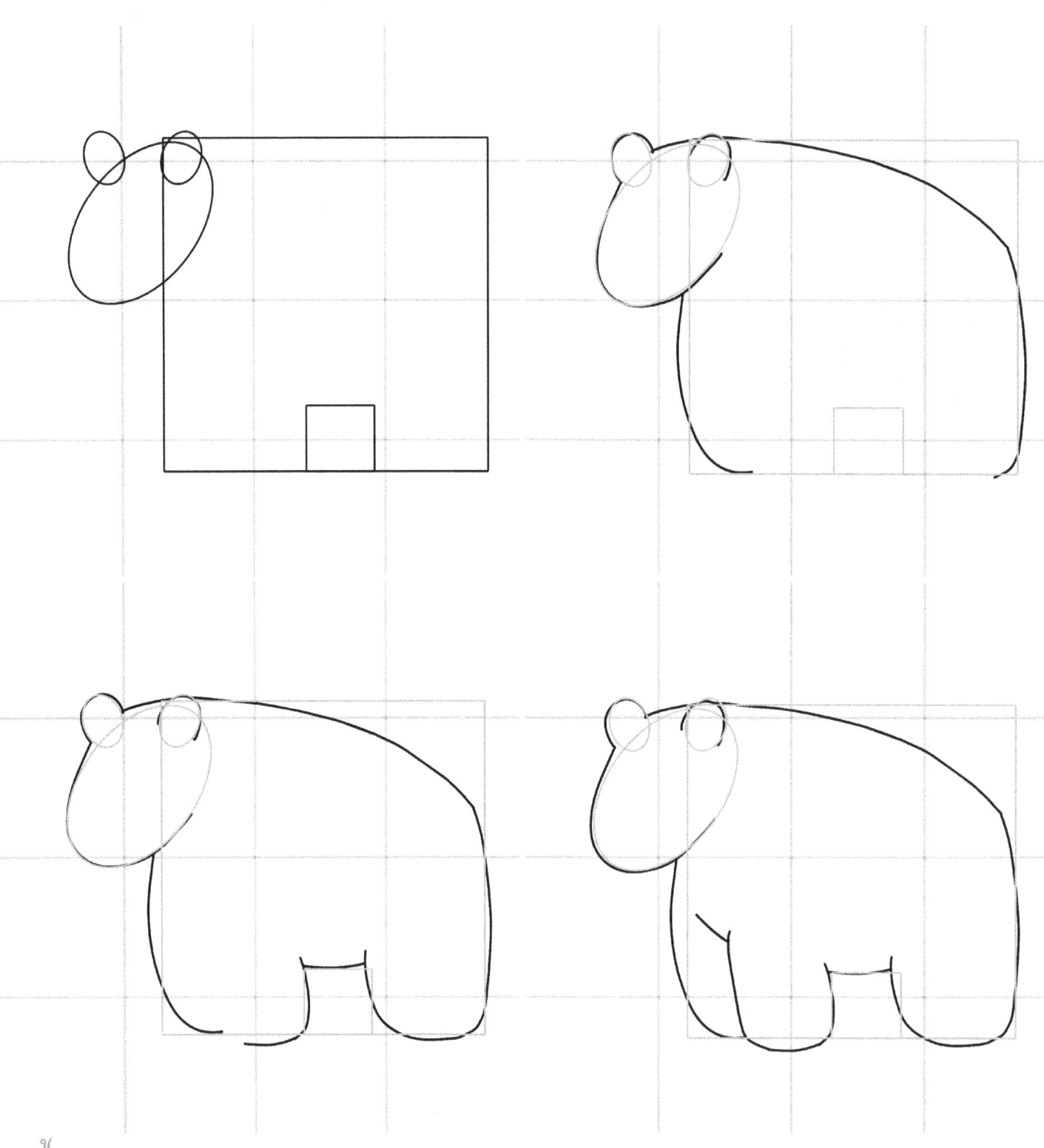

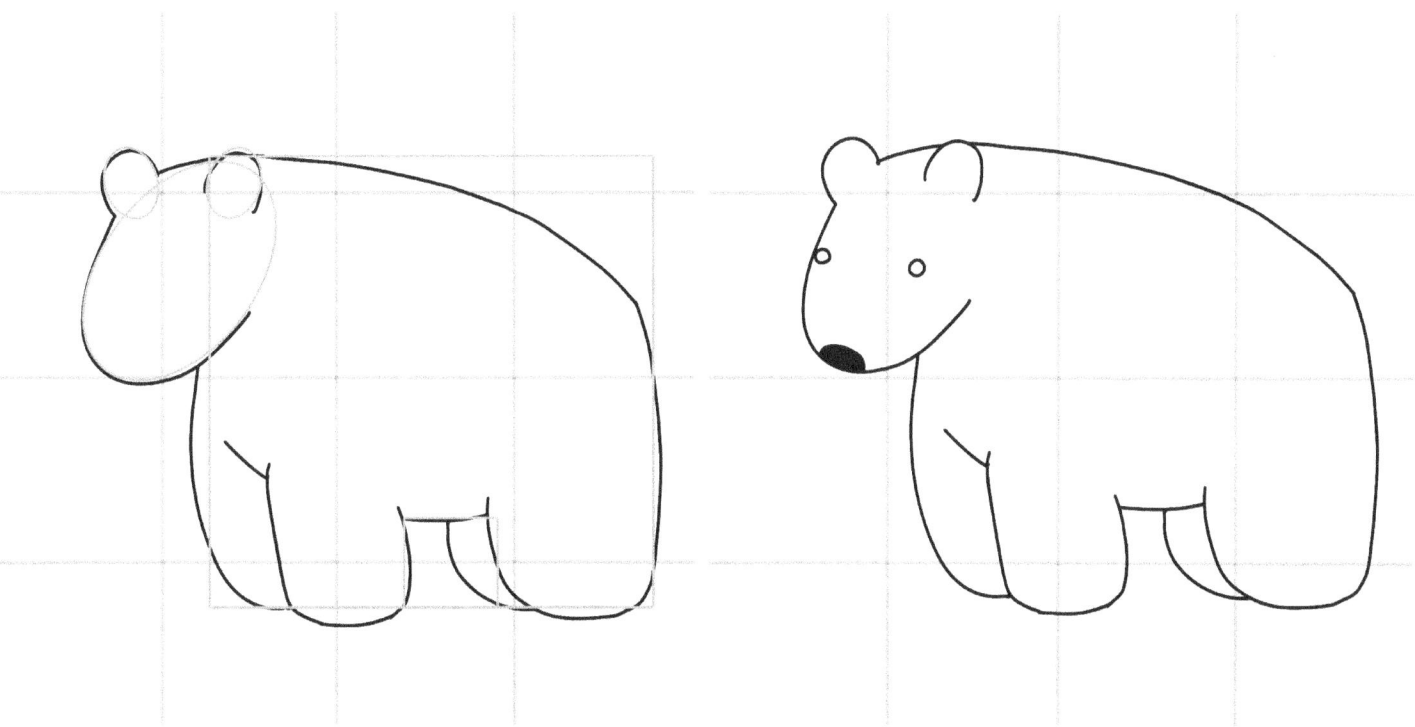

TRY it HERE!

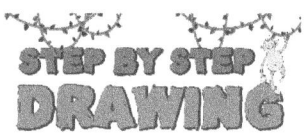

PUMA

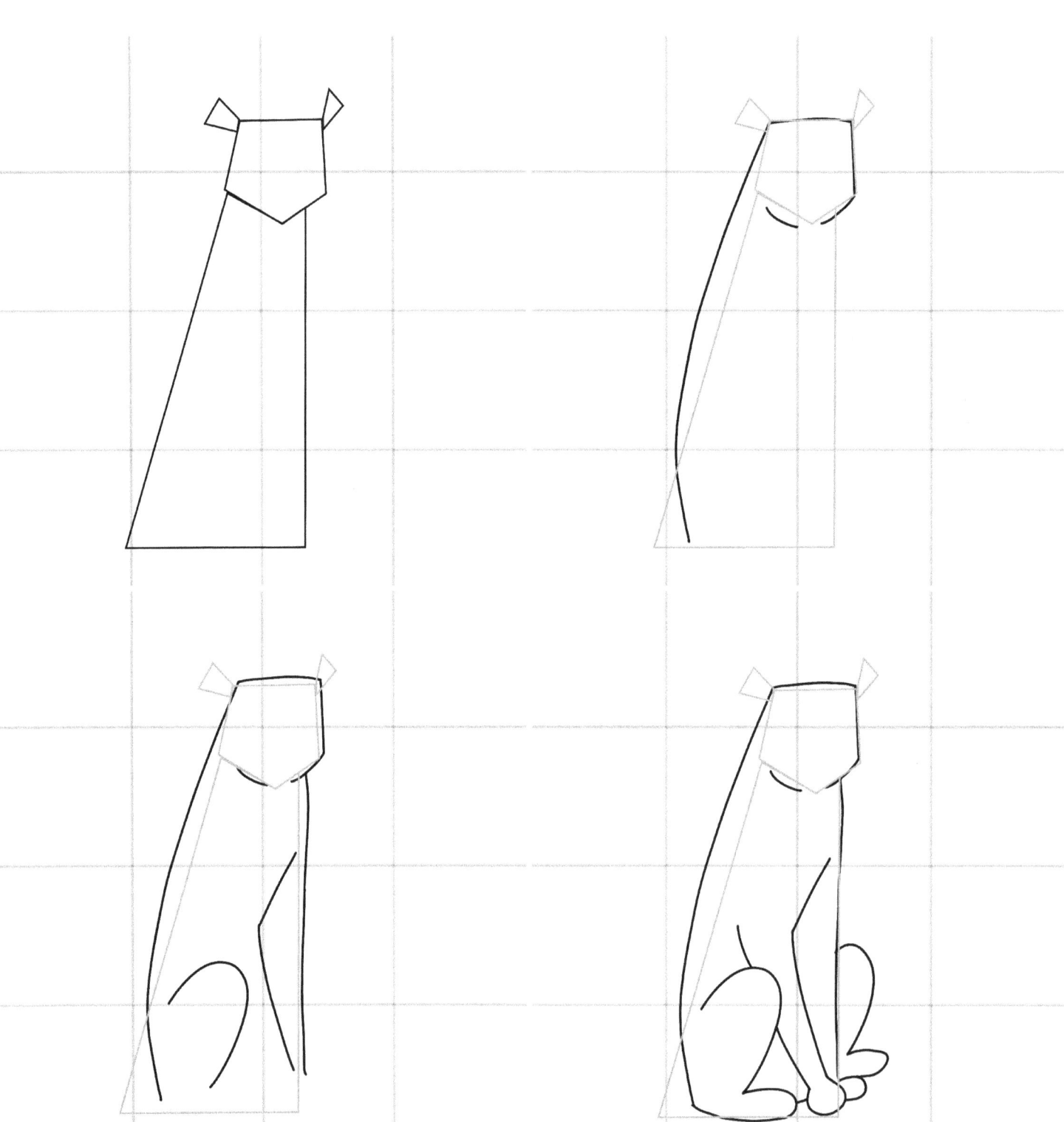

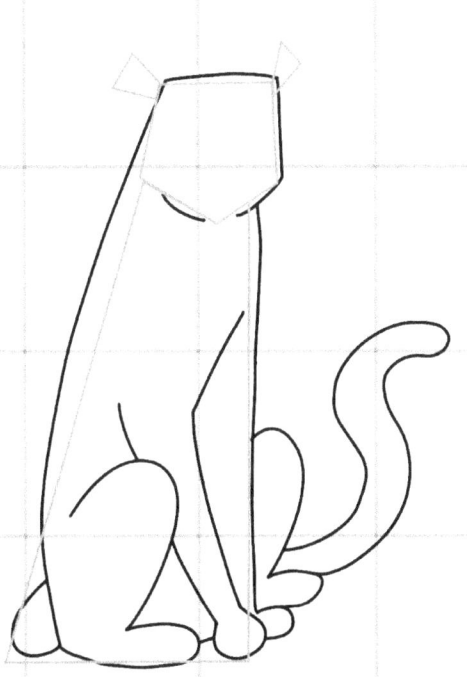

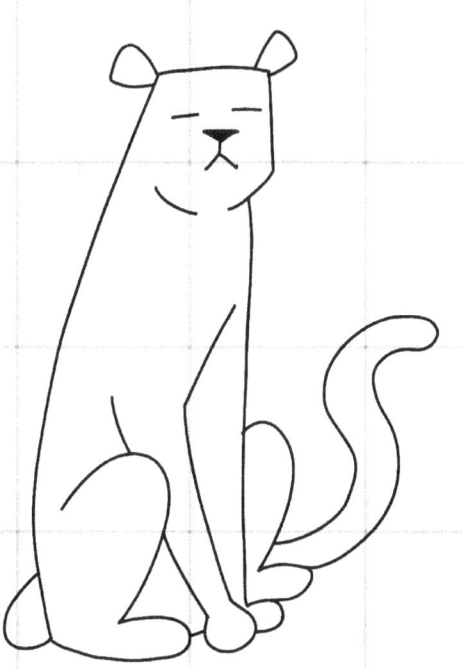

TRY it HERE!

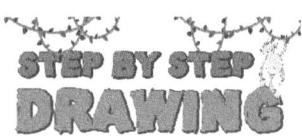

PUMA

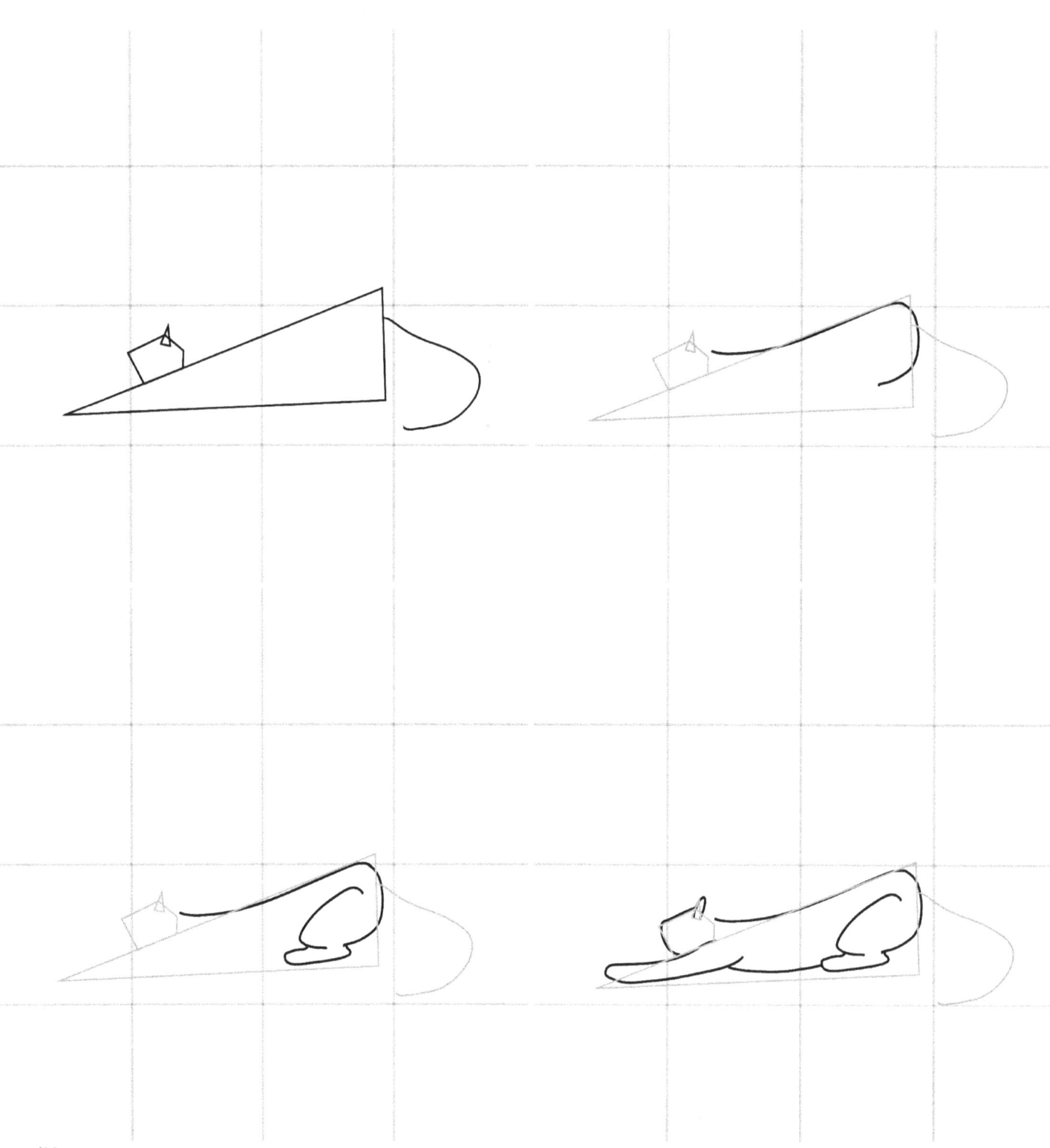

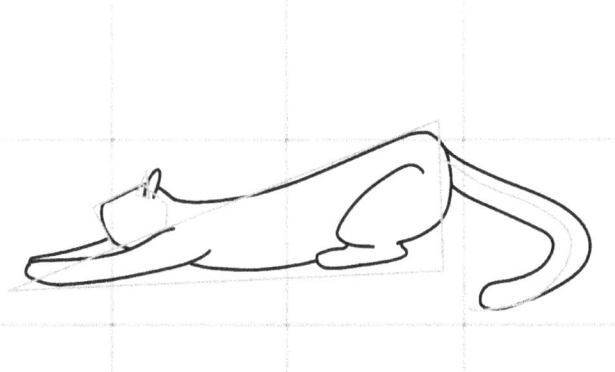
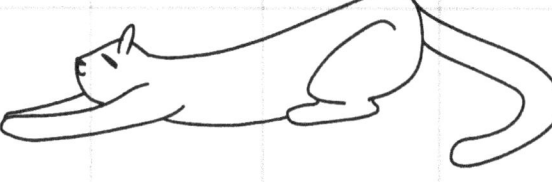

TRY it HERE!

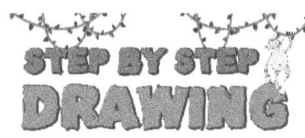

SLOTH

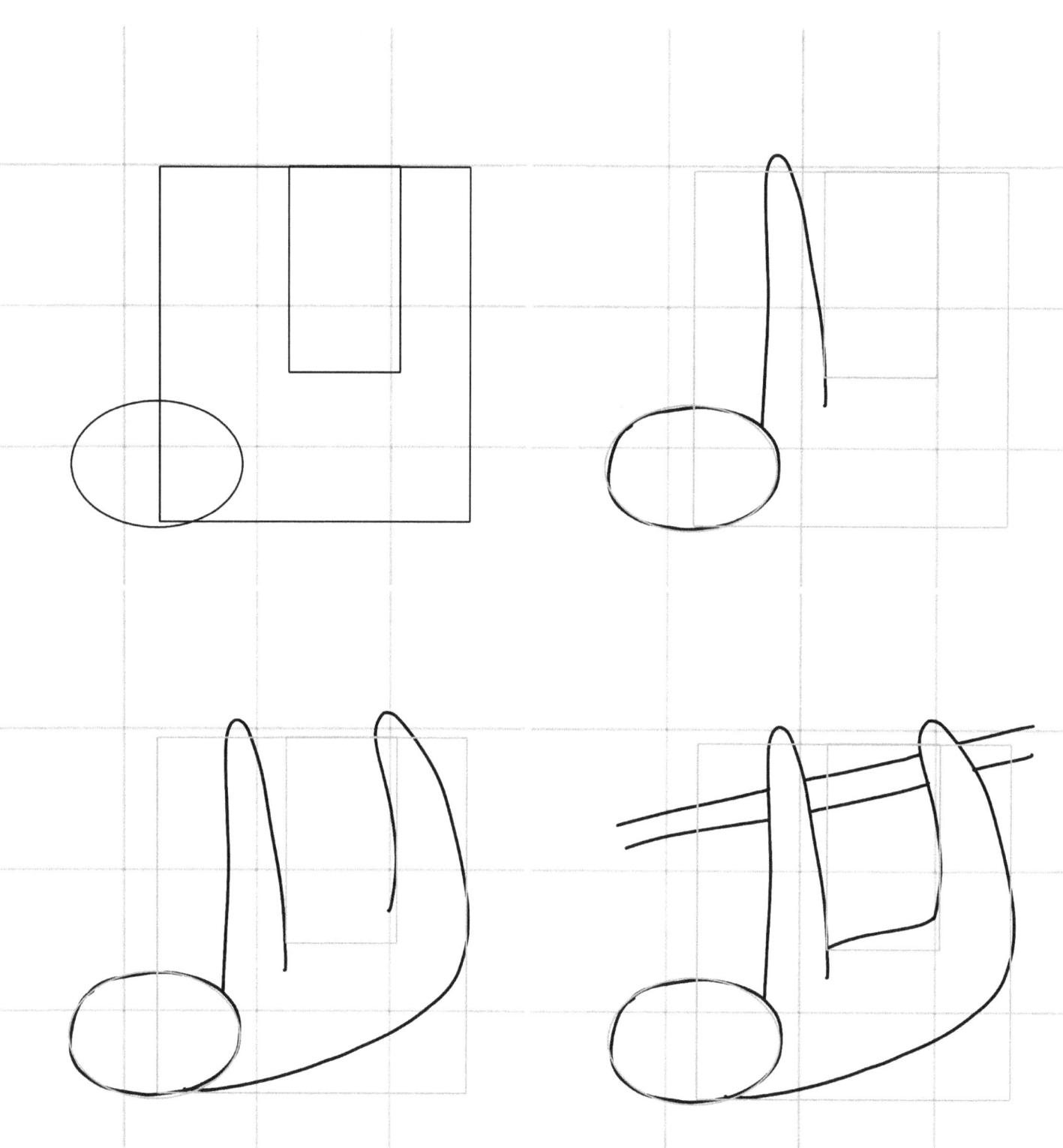

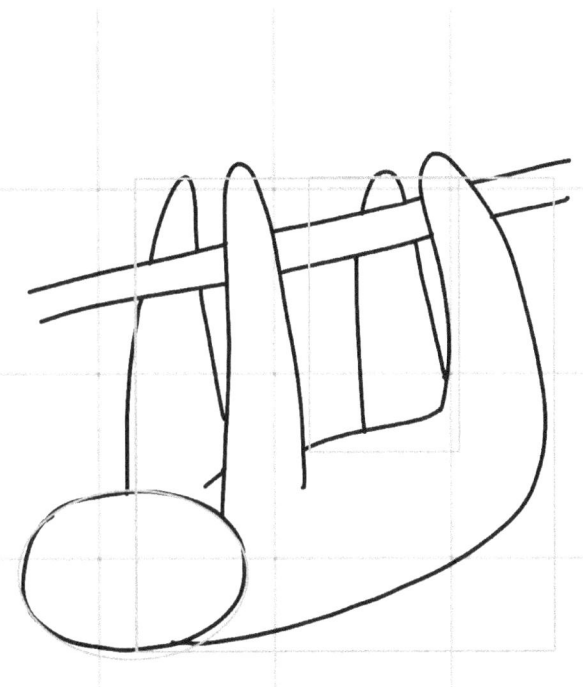

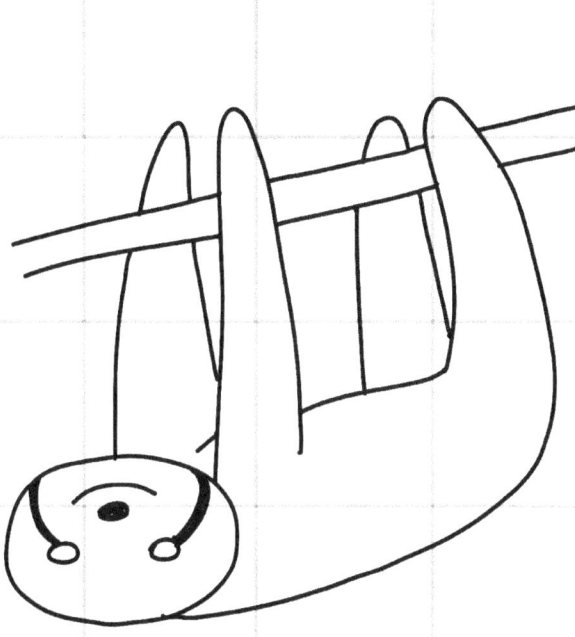

TRY it HERE!

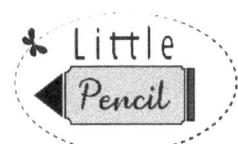
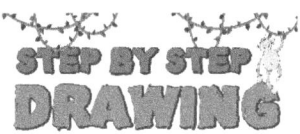

SLOTH

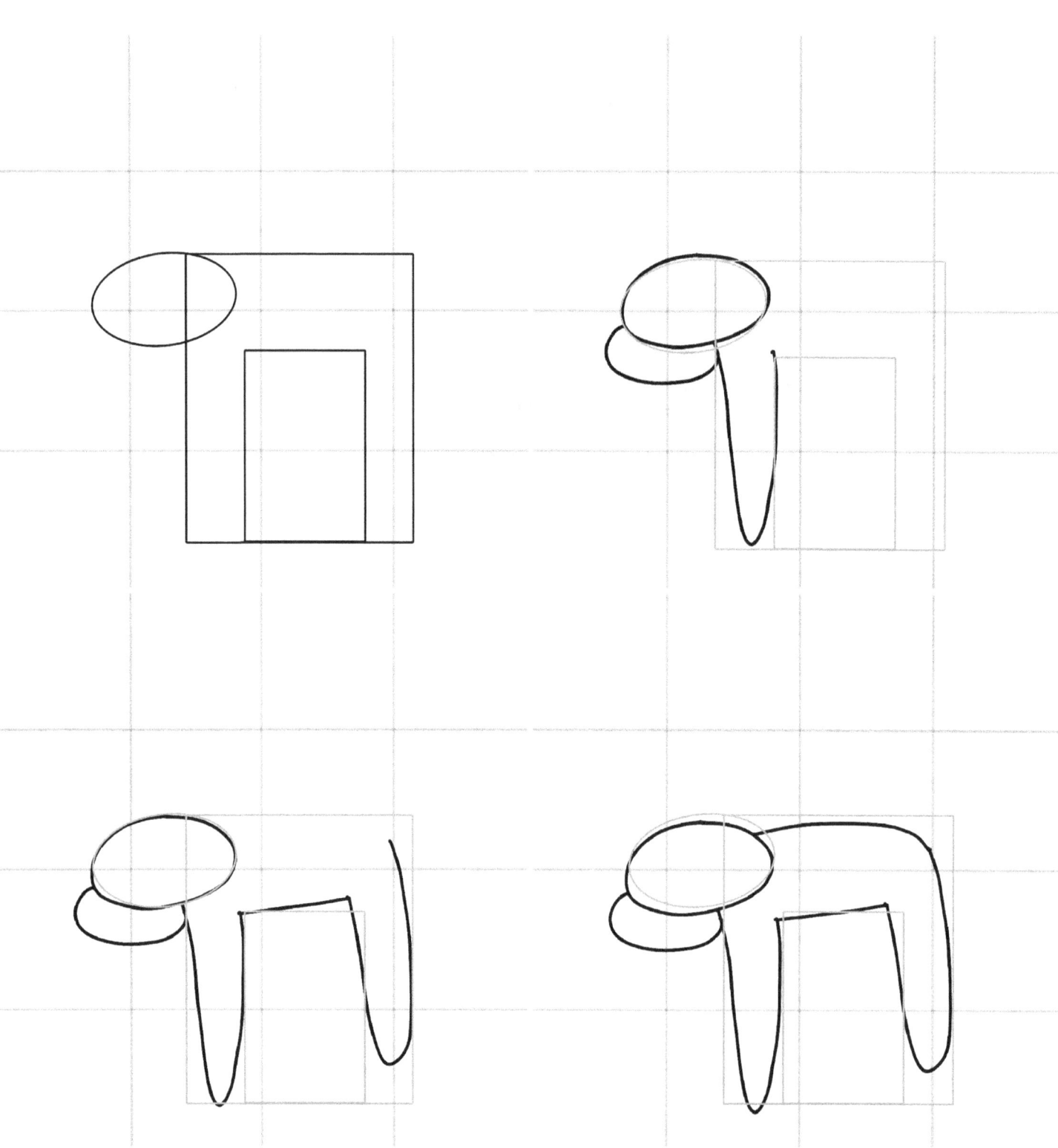

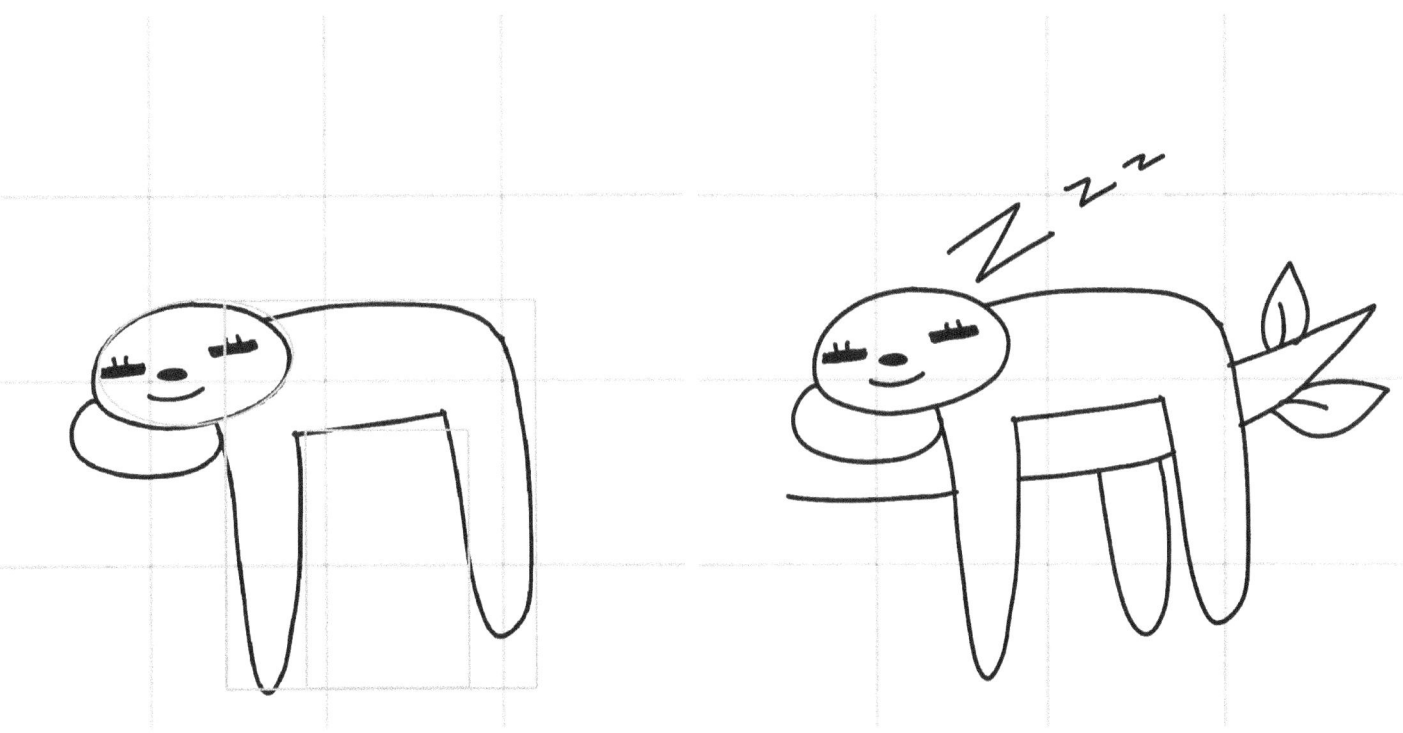

TRY it HERE!

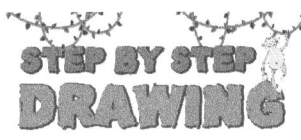

snake

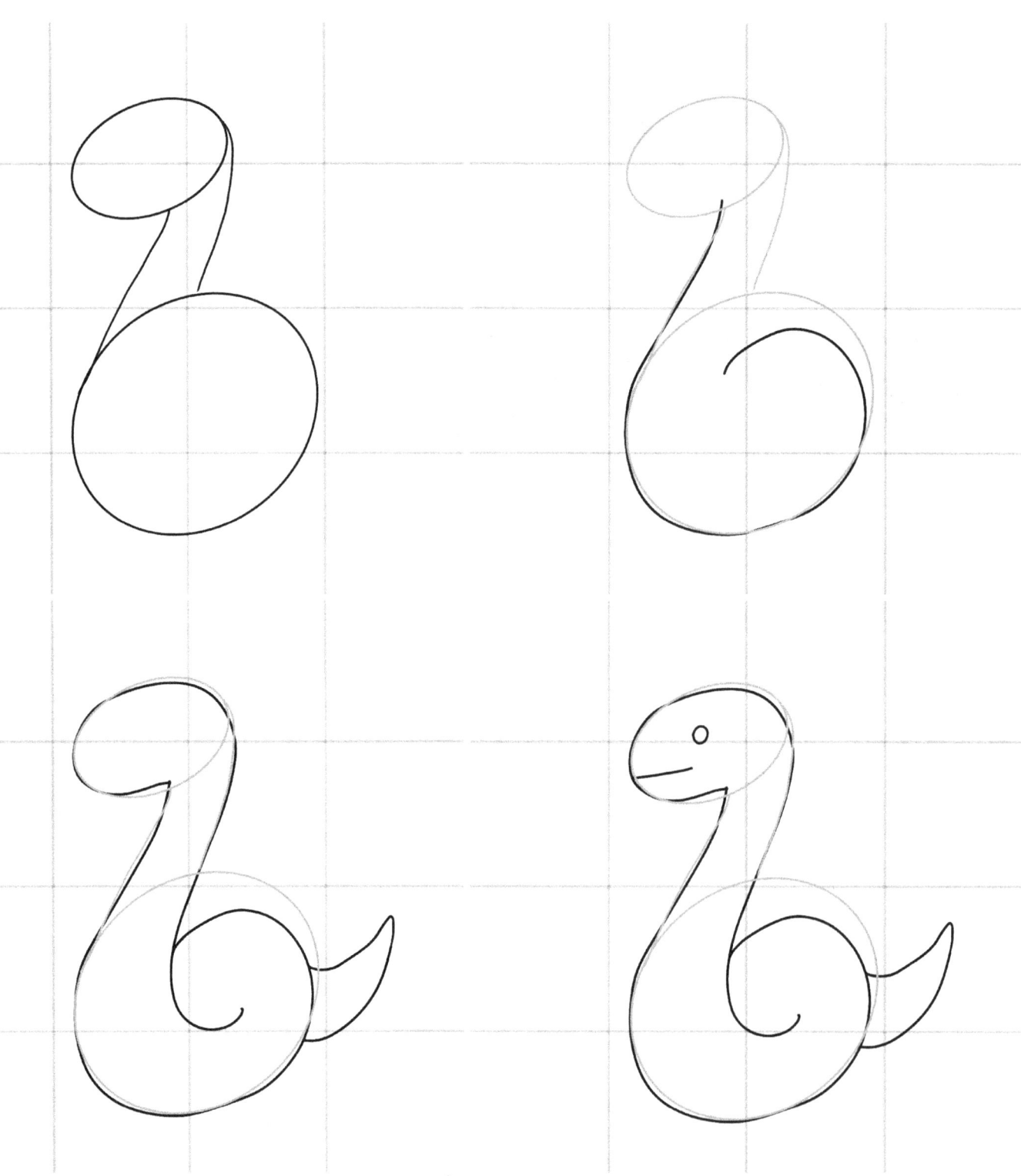

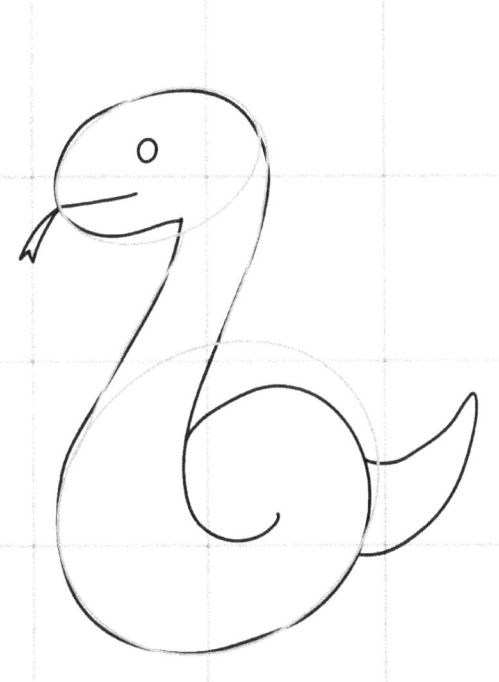

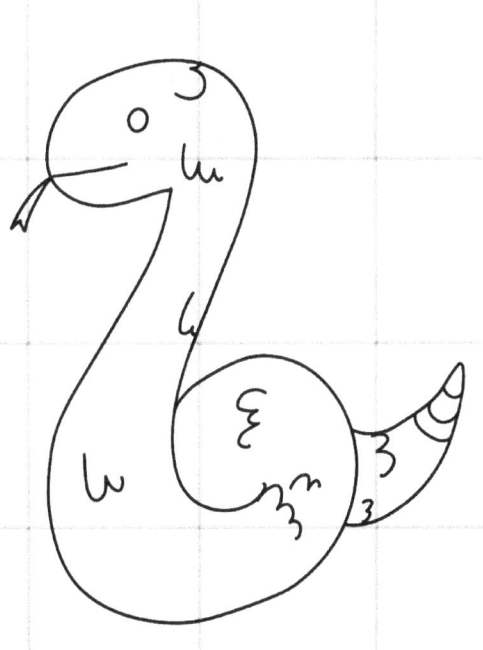

TRY it HERE!

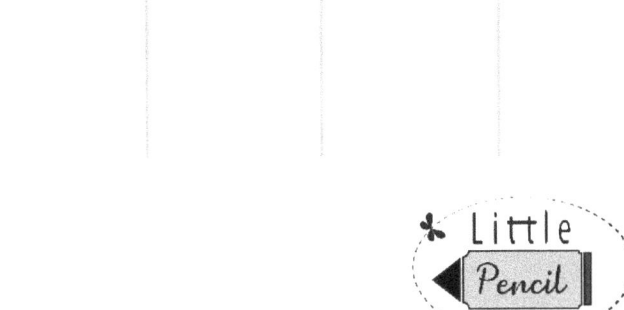
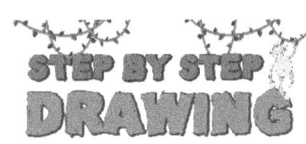

TIGER

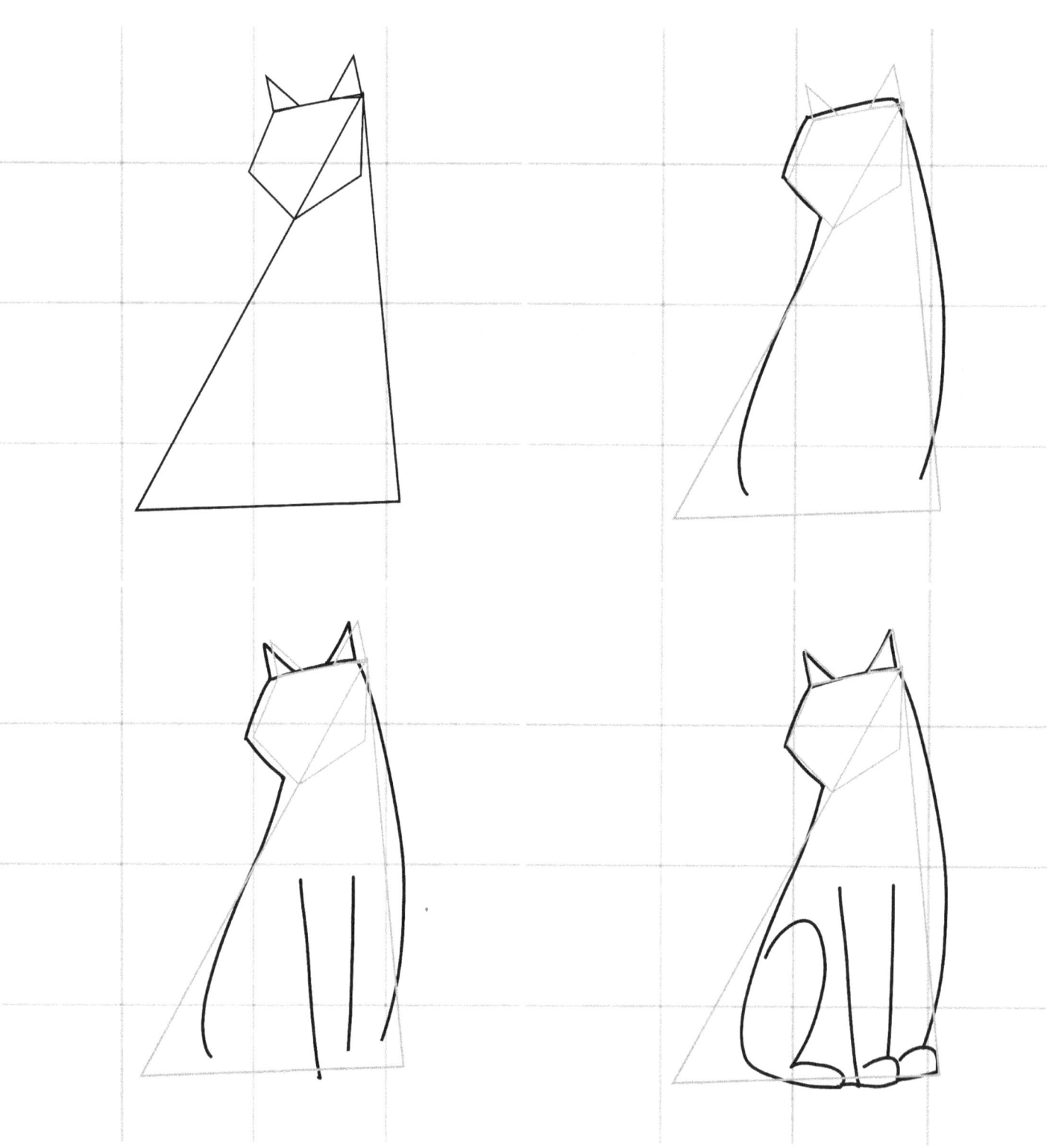

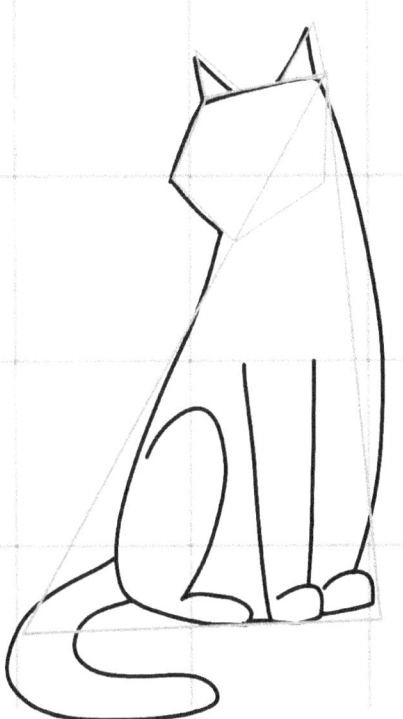
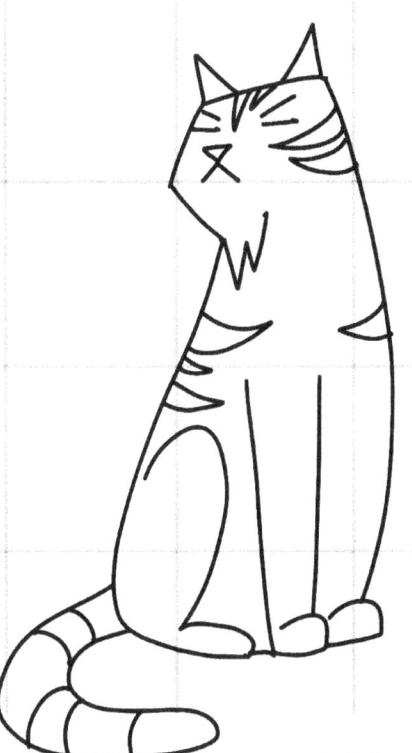

TRY it HERE!

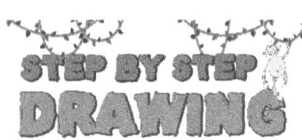

TOUCAN

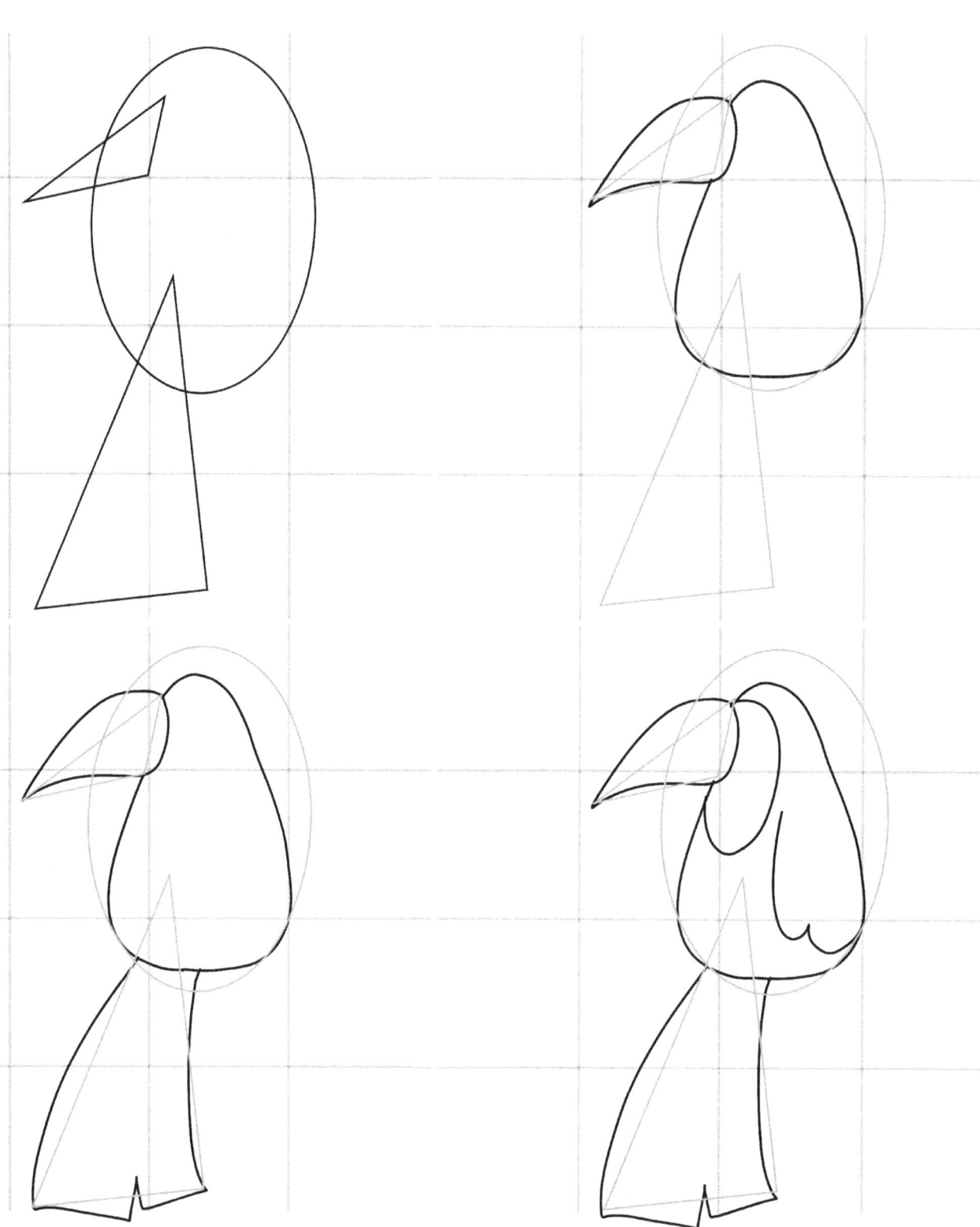

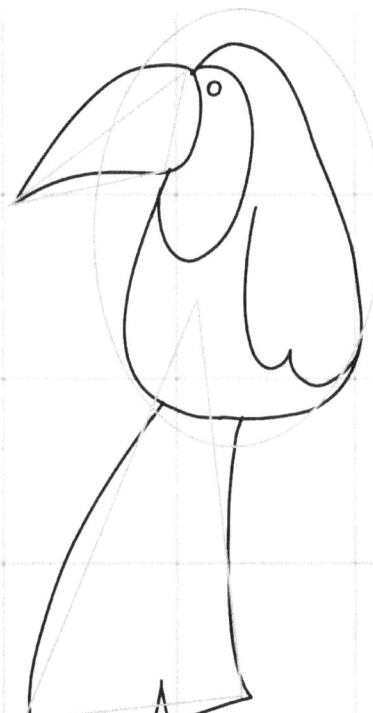

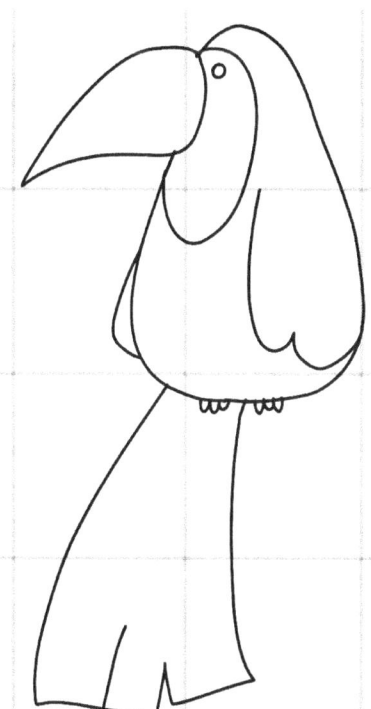

TRY it HERE!

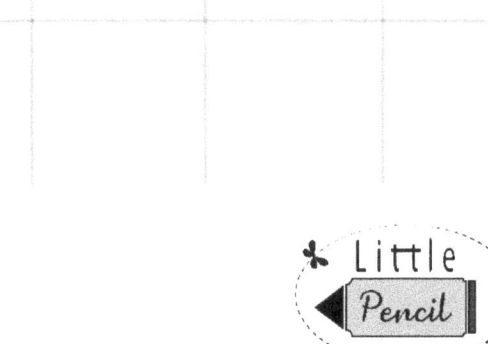
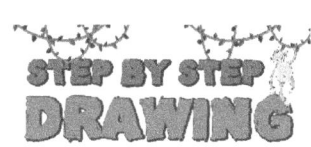

TREE FROG

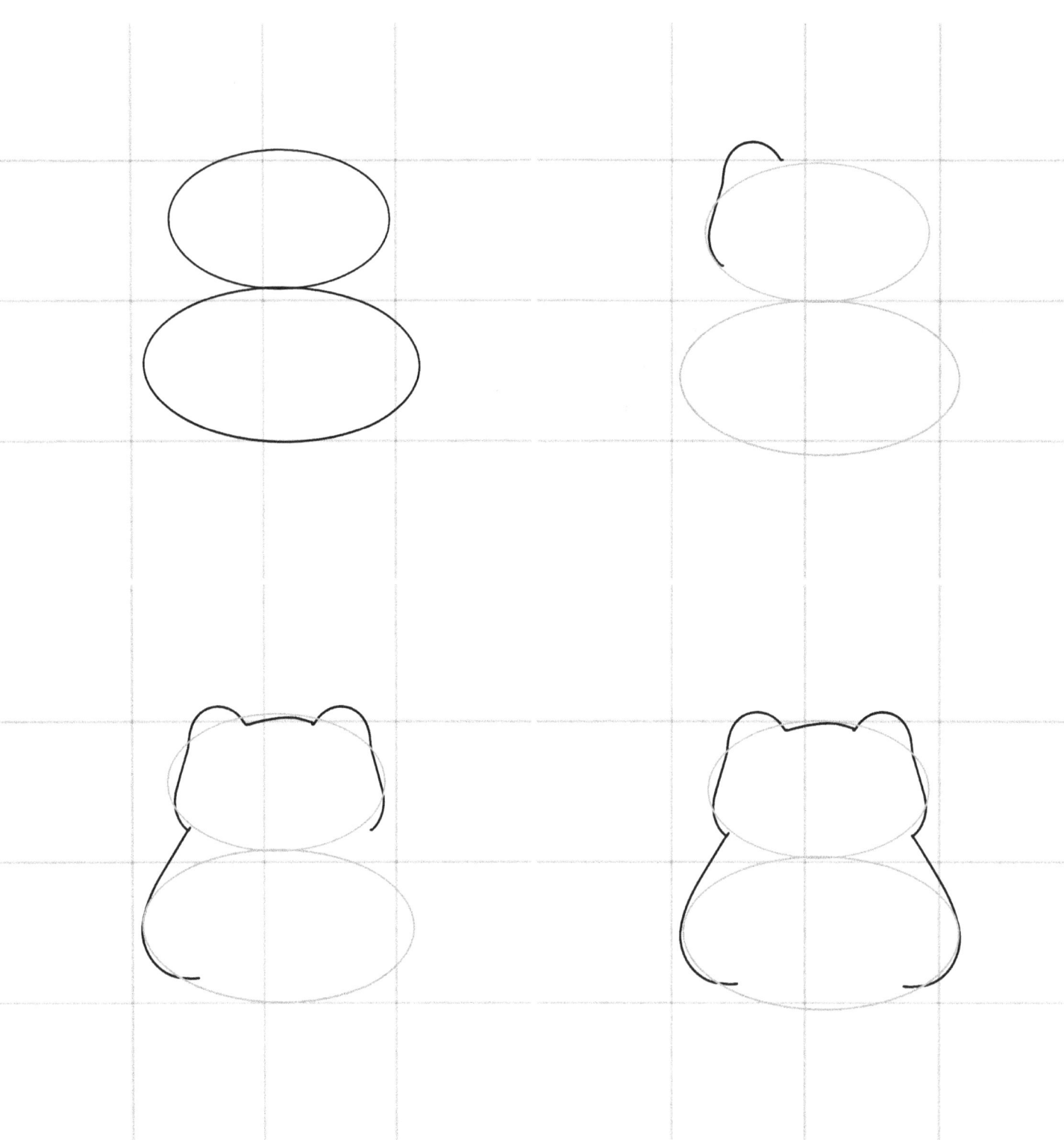

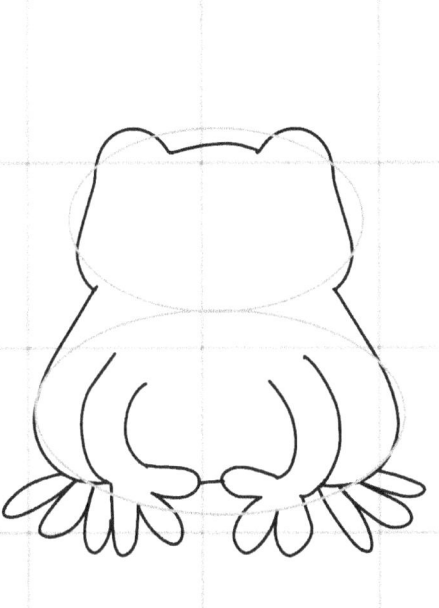
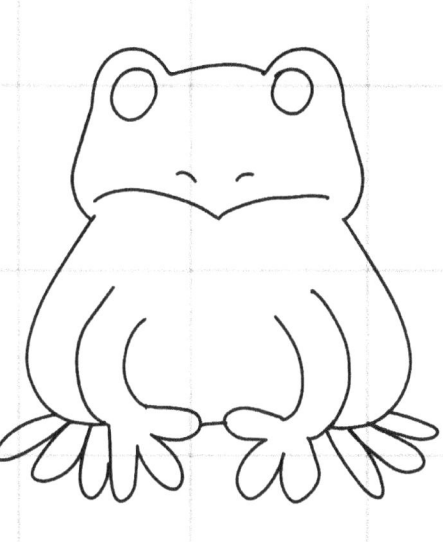

TRY iT HERE!

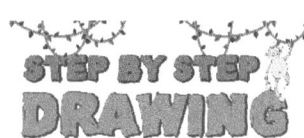

TURTLE

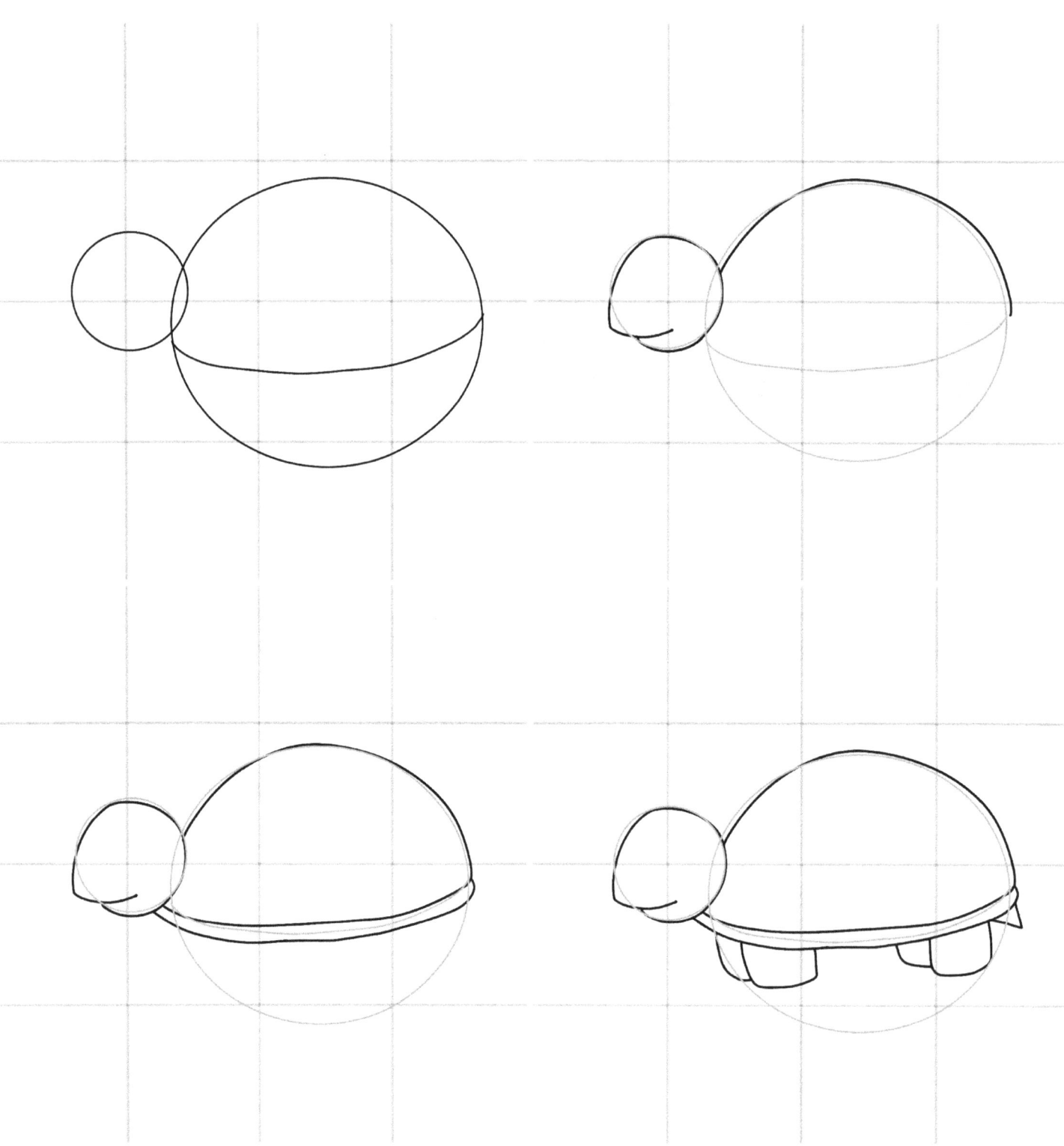

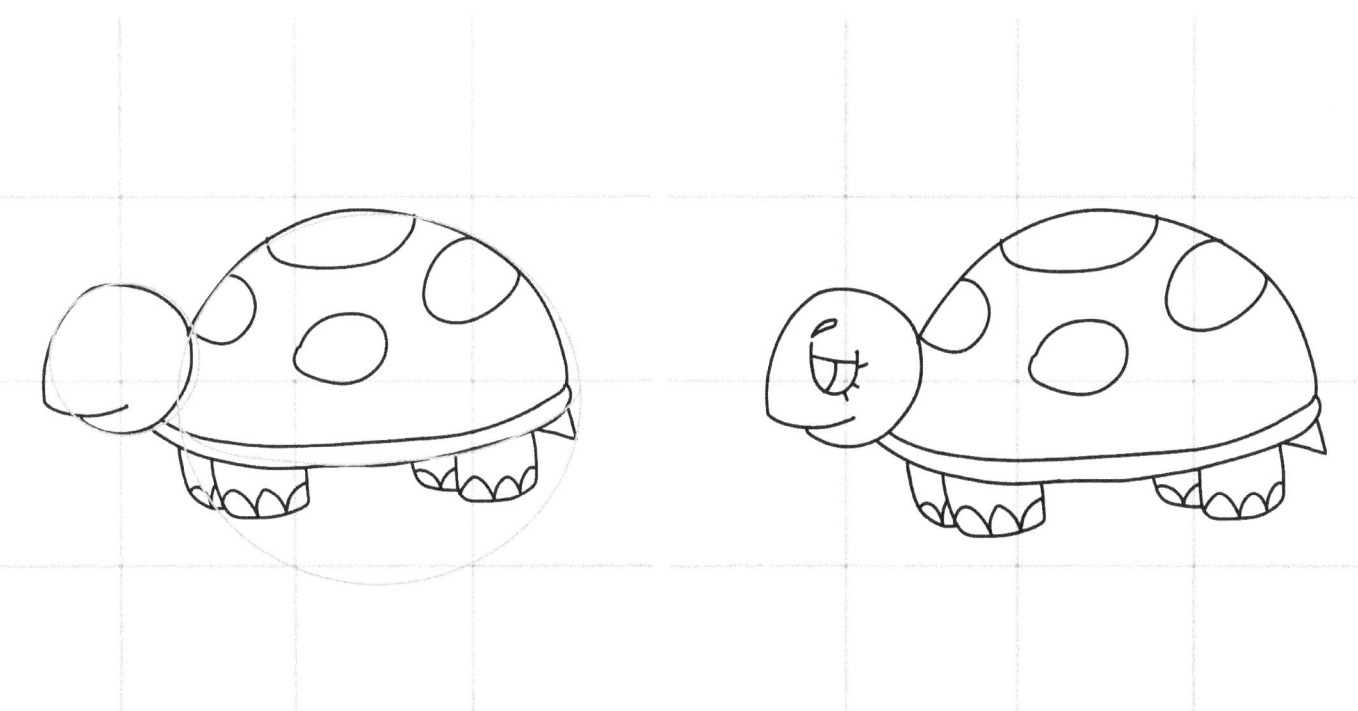

TRY it HERE!

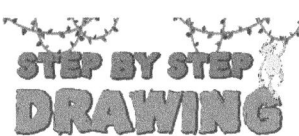

WALRUS

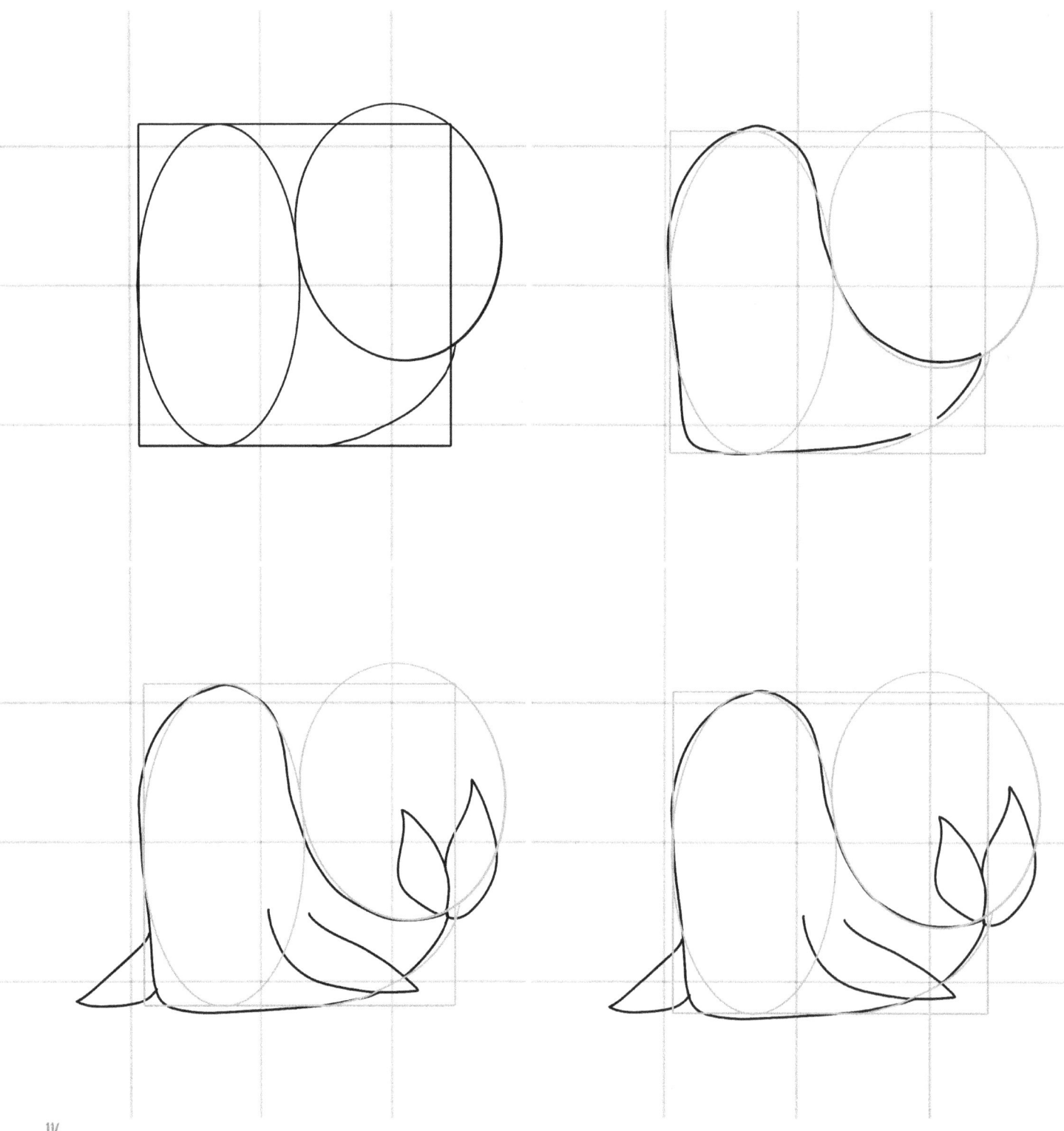

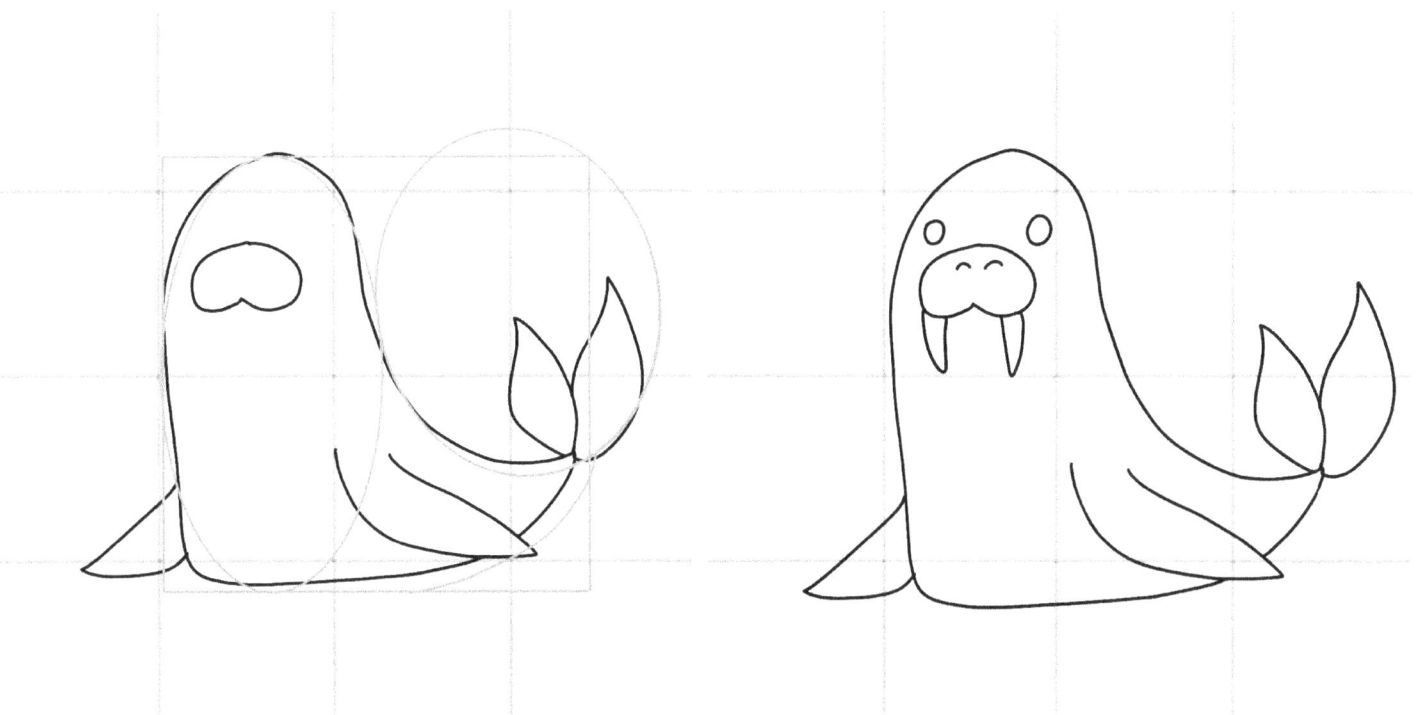

TRY it HERE!

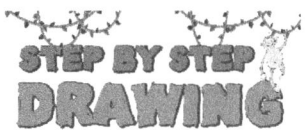

ZEBRA

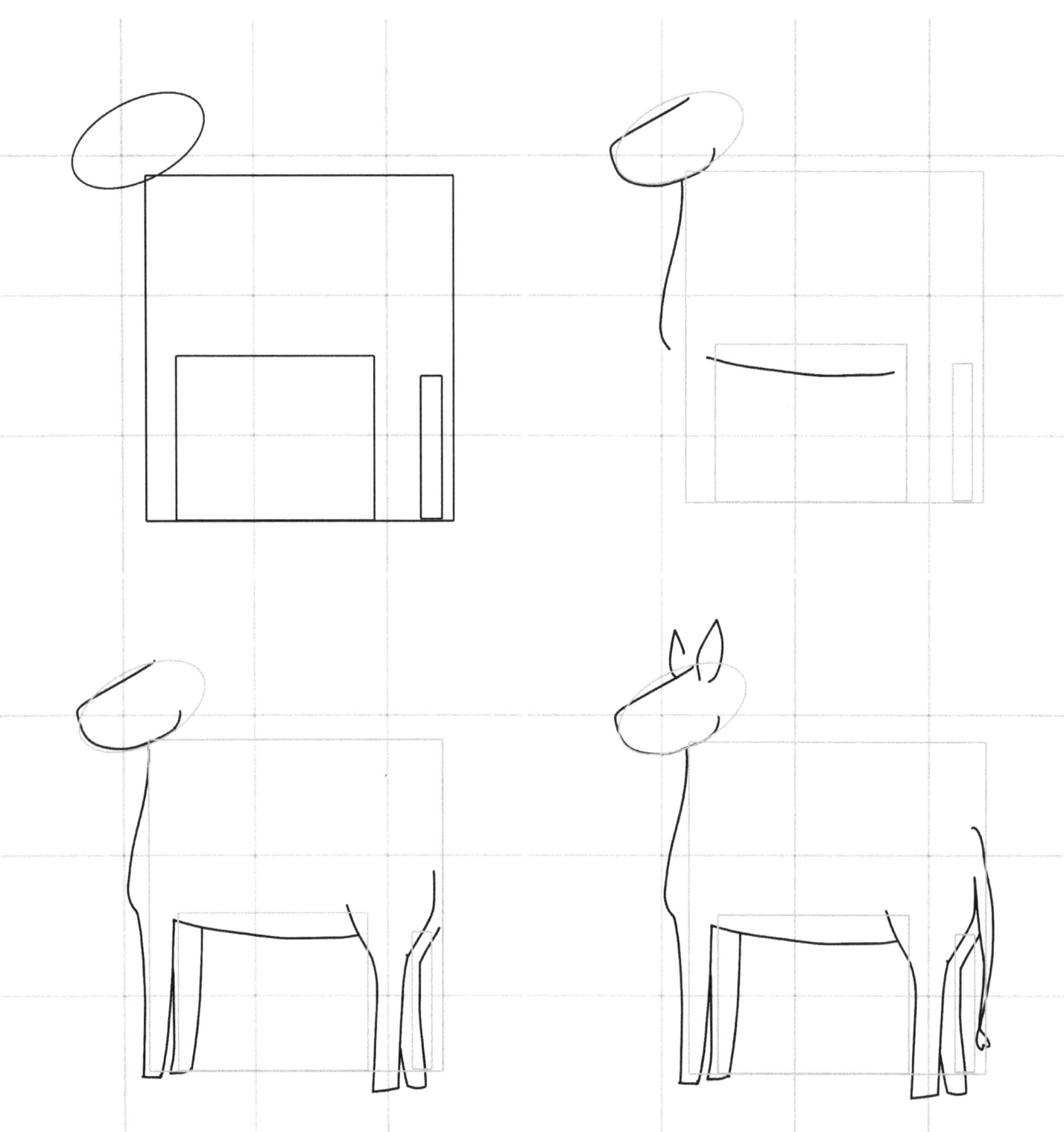

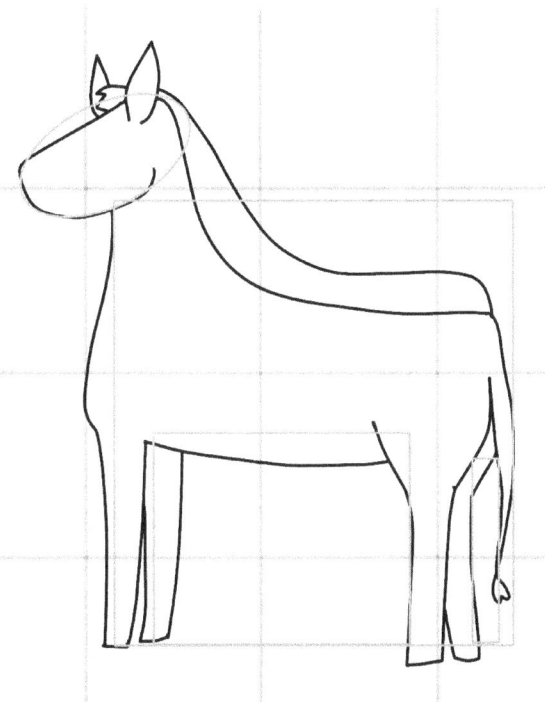

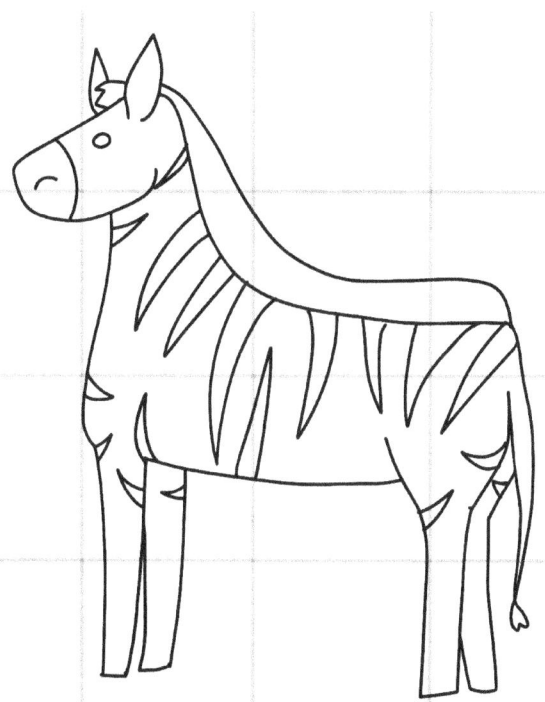

TRY it HERE!

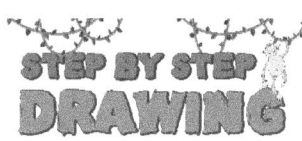

ABOUT THE AUTHOR

Miriam R. Ahumada

is a young illustrator that loves to draw and sing. Singing is a dream she still has time to pursue.

Miriam started drawing as a three-year-old thanks to his father and his T.V preferences, yeah, she liked watching the one, and only Bob Ross draw happy trees. Then when she was a little bit older, her inspiration became her cousin and her aunt Teresa, who showed her a lot of their own art when they were her age. Eventually she discovered Loish and decided to dive into digital art.

Miriam gathers inspiration from a lot of places and people like her own friends and other artists. She hopes that looking into this book as easy or difficult this drawing may seem,

you get the inspiration to create your own art and explore all you can do!

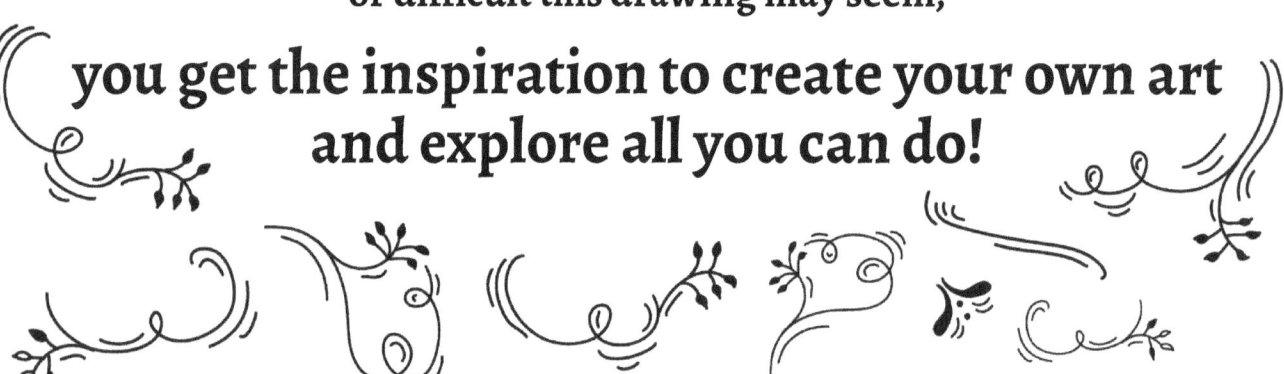

ACKNOWLEDGMENTS

A huge thank you to my family and to my friends, who inspire me daily with not only their art and great skills but with the perseverance and will to work the way they do. You are great artists, and I am lucky to call you all my friends.

A big thank you to every one of you that has given my book and myself the chance to guide you through this journey. The fact that you keep checking out my books makes me feel so special.

Practice and be patient with yourself and let your art speak through you.

If you have 20 seconds, please take a moment to leave a rating or review on Amazon, reviews really help us authors so much!

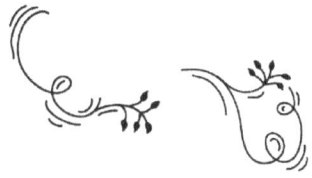
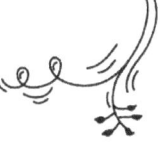

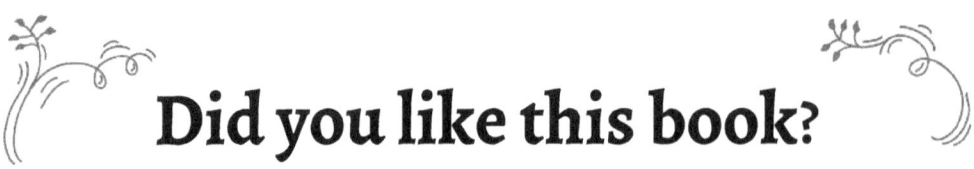

Did you like this book?

Be sure to check out the rest of

The Step by Step series by Little Pencil.

Keep practicing your awesome skills all the way from our wild Forest Animals to the depths of the Ocean, each with different difficulty levels!

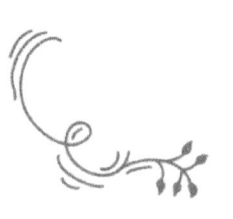

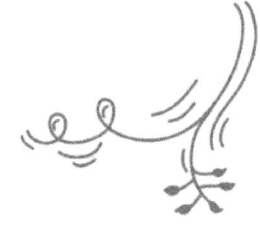

littlepencilpress.com

Scan this code and get some FREE extras!

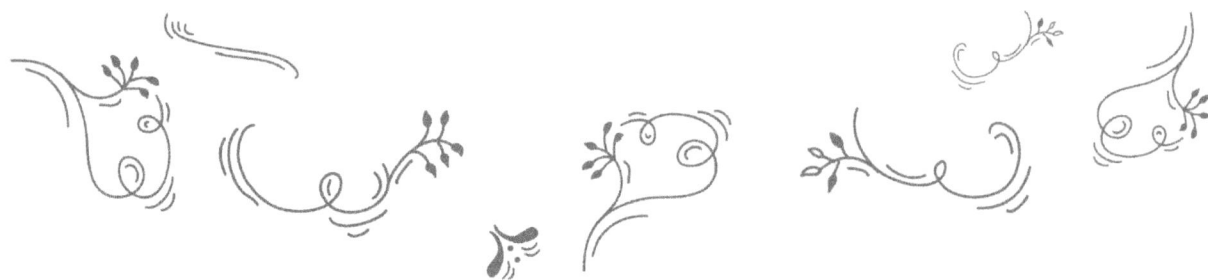

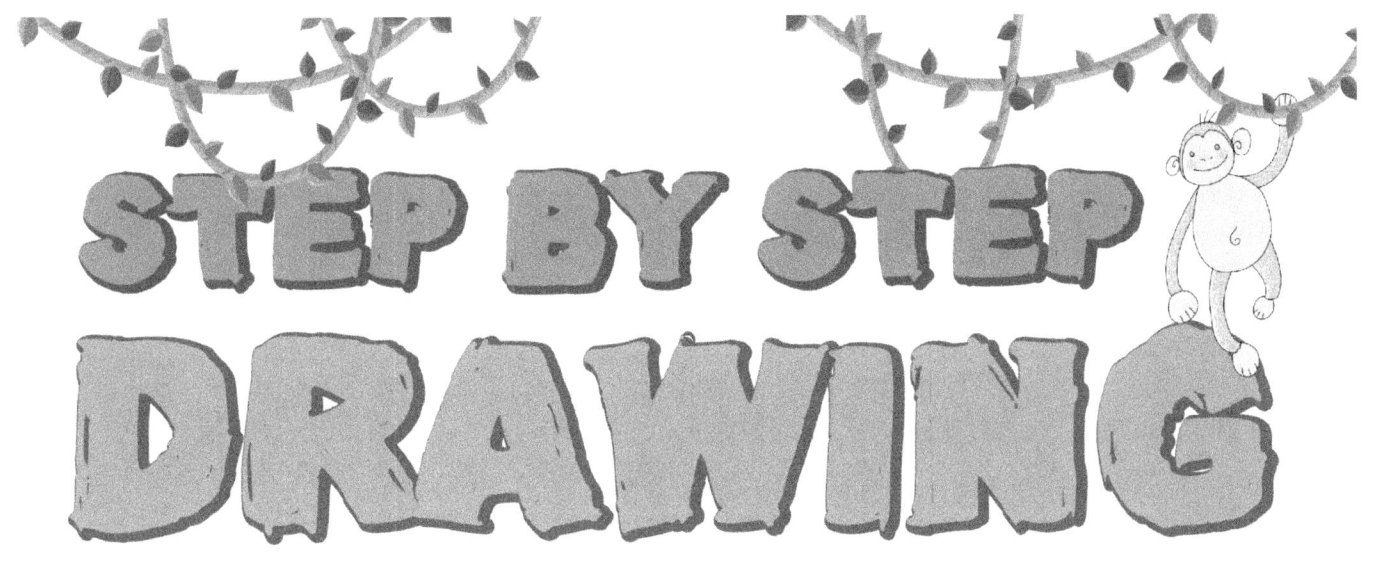